THE POWER OF MINDSET

THE POWER OF MINDSET

14 LIFE CHANGING PRINCIPLES ON HOW TO ACHIEVE TRUE HAPPINESS AND SUCCESS

HAYK TADEVOSYAN

FIREBRAND
PUBLISHING

Published by Firebrand Publishing Atlanta, GA USA

Firebrand Publishing publishes in a variety of print and electronic formats and by print-on-demand. For more information about Firebrand Publishing products, visit https://firebrandpublishing.com

ISBN: 978-1-649700-43-8 (cloth)

ISBN: 979-8-643914-57-0 (paperback)

ISBN: 978-1-941907-13-9 (ebook)

Printed in the United States of America

THANK YOU

I am Grateful for — family, health, friends, work and of course God for putting it all together for me!

Thank you to my wife Diana for being the voice of reason in my crazy life as it takes a very special person to in! uence my decisions and slow me down when I'm operating at an unsustainable speed. Thank you for blessing me with the most valuable gift a husband can ask for, the gift of becoming a father. I couldn't have asked for a better gift in life than the two boys you have blessed me with, David and Arman.

Thank you to my sister Hripsime and brother Albert for teaching and serving as examples of what a good brother and a sister should be. I am lucky to have siblings that I can also call my best friends. I also want to thank my mentors, friends, my irreplaceable team and peers for supporting me, pushing me, occasionally dragging me back to reality and always being there for me. I am blessed to be surrounded by such valuable people in my life, that I value immensely.

I would like to dedicate this book to my parents Yuri and Mariam. They were my very first mentors. They risked everything they had built and worked for, moved to the United States of America to give me, my brother and my sister a privileged opportunity they never had growing up. Words cannot express my gratitude for all of the sacrifices they have made for us. The word lucky doesn't begin to describe how fortunate I am, for having the parents that I do. They are the reason why today, I am in the position to write this book and enjoy the wonderful benefits of my life.

Thank you,
Hayk

CONTENTS

PREFACE

First, a Confession.

Initially, I did not start writing this book for others, nor did I want to share my writings with anyone. I started writing a journal for myself.

My life's experiences, thoughts, ideas, philosophy, principles and out of the box thinking, has always been something that I was too afraid to express. So, for the longest time, I kept it all in my head. When the time was right, I decided to get it all out on paper, so I'm not up at three in the morning brainstorming lessons, thoughts and ideas. I wanted to get it all out for myself so I could have easy access to it all, versus wondering what the great idea was that I'd had in the middle of night.

As I started dumping my mind onto paper, my thoughts started becoming clearer. Sentences turned into paragraphs, paragraphs turned into pages, pages became chapters and with hundreds of written pages, I realised that I needed to share my lessons with the world.

At first, there was way too much; I needed a way to clarify and categorise the information. So I narrowed it all down to 14 lessons, which is how the 14 Principles were born.

The 14 Principles will guide you towards a balanced successful life, and will help you understand and develop habits of continuous success with purpose. If you have ever enjoyed temporary success in the past, and wondered how to replicate a more consistent and sustainable lifestyle for the future, then what I share in this book will be of great benefit.

This book will serve as a manual to the basics of a healthy mind, and a purposeful life. Everything is at your fingertips; and it all comes down to your mindset.

The 14 principles will guide you through the basic stages of mental push-ups, to help you become a more capable person. The Power of Mindset does not need to be read in order. Rather, it contains a number of small and big lessons that will spark a fire in your mind, so feel free to skip chapters, read ahead and come back to them, as all 14 Principles are connected, but not in any specific order.

I wrote this book with a goal of helping you develop a stronger sense of self, and find balance with four distinct areas of your life that are essential for your success - Family, Fitness, Friendships and Finances.

"Whether you think you can or you think you can't, you are right." - Henry Ford

INTRODUCTION

"The more you know, the more you know you don't know."
-Aristotle

I fell in love with this quote by Aristotle in my late twenties. I wish I had learned the lesson from this quote sooner. I began to understand that it is solely myself, who should be blamed, or praised, for all my decision and its outcomes in my life. The older I got, the wiser I became, and the wiser I became, the more I realised how much I *don't* know. Not only about the world, but about myself. As I was becoming more aware I was beginning to understand that life's conditions never come before the mindset.

I learned that things that can be purchased never actually brought happiness - only temporary satisfaction. I learned the happy and successful people that I admired were already happy *way* before they obtained all their material conditions.

With this book I want to share my findings and my story with those who like to learn from others. As William Prescott, the commander of the patriot forces in the Battle of Bunker Hill once said, *"Some people learn by the mistakes of others, but most of us are the others."*

Learning from our mistakes is a never-ending cycle that makes us who we are. We don't live long enough to make all the necessary mistakes to learn from, which is why learning from others is so important. If I was happy or unhappy with a relationship, I traced it back to an emotional decision I made in the past, which led to how that relationship was today.

If I was satisfied or unsatisfied with my health, I reflected on decisions I made concerning diet and exercise that led to my health today. Similarly, the way I felt about my finances, was due to a decision involving my career, risk, or education I'd made previously, that had led to my current situation with money.

Every decision we make, good or bad, intentional or unintentional, always comes with consequences. Often, it's easier to accept where we are today and who we have become, and to acknowledge that our current condition is a result of the decisions we've made in the past. The small daily choices we make over time, become our reality today. While there is not much we can do about yesterday, today is ours so we can influence tomorrow.

Let's make a better tomorrow, today.

From birth to eighteen years old, my family relocated twelve times between three different countries. Armenia, Russia and the United States. We often moved around for one purpose, to find financial stability. While I was growing up, putting food on the table regularly was an obstacle in my home country of Armenia. The aftermath of the Soviet Union collapse had led to government corruption, and the only option to support a family for many people, was to look for work in other countries. Moving so many times from place to place in an effort to find financial solidity, gave me a strong perspective on my objective in life.

Like most of us, I was made to believe during my childhood years that the ultimate source of happiness is money, and that it's the "panacea" for all our struggles. So, I worked very hard and early on accomplished financially, what many people don't in a lifetime. By the time I was in my early twenties, I had already owned two businesses generating six-figure residual income that continued to increase every year. I can't ignore the fact that money did solve a lot of issues like having a stable roof over my head, buying food, affording electricity and medicine but money did also come with an empty feeling of dissatisfaction. So, in broad strokes, no, money doesn't equal happiness, but it equals a solid foundation from which I could reach for happiness.

I owned and operated a very high-producing insurance and financial services agency in Bellevue, Washington, the same city where the Microsoft home office is located. So you can imagine, obtaining clients with money wasn't an issue.

My second gig was a construction business, which did extremely well during the huge real estate boom in the East Seattle area. I ran both businesses out of my office in Bellevue. Right in the center of all the action.

By the time I was in my mid to late twenties, I already had rental properties, a nice house, sports cars and couldn't spend my money fast enough. What I was especially proud of was the fact that I had built my business into a self-sustaining machine that no longer needed my physical presence. My system and team ran the entire business for me. Each year, I would work less, but make more money, which at times felt too good to be true. I assumed I would feel secure, happy and successful by having what I never had growing up: financial stability.

What my family had chased for so long was an illusion of success. I, of course, appreciated being able to make a steady living and support both my parents and my struggling relatives in my home country. However, it was not what drove happiness into my life. Even though I knew I wouldn't have to worry about money ever again, I felt in no way successful during that time.

As a matter of fact, I felt empty and unaccomplished, which was really odd because the decades of financial struggle were finally over for my family. But the empty thirst and desire for success never went away. Somehow, my thirst wasn't quenched.

I began to look at other areas of my life that lacked success. I started to understand the importance of health in my mid-20s, and implemented consistent activities and a good diet, as the workload of the early stage of my businesses took a toll on my health. In my late 20's, I discovered how critical a part of life family is. I married my best friend Diana, who later blessed me with two of the best boys in the world.

This was when I truly felt like I was the most successful man on earth despite the fact that I wasn't the wealthiest, healthiest, had the biggest family, or the most friends. Yet, I had found what I had been searching for my entire life, a healthy BALANCE of family, fitness, friendships and finances.

The Power of Mindset outlines the epiphany I had, that brought together all the pieces of the puzzle, that my family spent a lifetime looking for. I felt like I had struck gold. However, when I look back over what got me finally feeling successful, I realized they were a result of my purposeful effort, and self-discipline.

I turned those lessons into these 14 Principles.

Before we get into the meat of the lessons, consider the following analogy. Let's imagine a world where you can set your mind to pick up any radio station frequency, just by thought. If you have read Napoleon Hill's *Think and Grow Rich*, or followed Albert Einstein's law of Vibrations Research, you know that everything vibrates. You can pick up the frequency with your mind, just like you would when tuning into a radio station on your stereo.

For example, there are the happy, sad, positive, negative, success or failure frequencies. Let's say you are looking to hear the status of your favorite football team's game, so you tune into the appropriate AM station. However, if you are on the FM frequency, you will never find the information you're looking for, no matter how hard you try, unless you manually turn the knob. So why don't we manually tune our minds to the frequency we want?

How do we tune into attracting good, success, positivity, health, intentional relationships, financial gain, and more?

Why do other people get positive results, even when giving far less resources?

The answer is, your MINDSET. Your own ability to control your habits, which influences your mind and gives you the ability to more easily control the frequency you should be tuned into, and avoid the frequencies you shouldn't.

But of course, this is easier said than done.

After all, how do you gain control over something that you *don't* have much control over, but thought you did? If we had complete control over our minds, we would live in a perfect world where goals are a reality, and success in all categories was a part of everyday life, and no longer something we strive for. Having no control is normal, because it means we are imperfect, which is something we as society, need to get better at accepting. This leads us to set goals.

We don't just set goals so we can *achieve* them. Part of setting goals is the journey of getting there, and the process of growth that happens along the way. Healthy progress is more beneficial, mentally and physically, than achieving the goal that kicked off the process to begin with.

Think about it, if a runner sets a goal to run ten miles in 60 minutes, the long-term positive gain on the health and discipline, is so much more considerable on the body and mind than the actual 60-minute record. The record is set one time, but the long-term positive outcome from all the training, not to mention the habits formed, can remain for a lifetime.

Goals are what we set out to achieve through step-by-step action. Although we may not get exactly what we want, the *process* of what we learn while on that path, betters us a million times more than the achievement.

Let's go back to the runner example. Let's say the closest you got is 80 minutes for a 10-mile run. If that's better than what you began with, then you're already considerably healthier, and in better physical and mental shape. The process led to a lower resting heart rate, a better working conditioned system, a more disciplined mind, and a faster metabolism.

Just because you didn't achieve that 60-minute goal does not mean you failed. You can apply this same logic to *any* process or goal. The outcome has nothing to do with losing or winning. Achieving any level of improvement is a positive outcome, regardless of whether or not the initial goal was met.

So, does anyone know how their mind works? Can anyone control their mind?

There are a lot of research out there on how we only use 10% of our brain, while 90% remains untapped. Scientific American published a great article on this subject on February 7, 2008 written by Robynne Boyd referencing neurologist Barry Gordon at Johns Hopkins School of Medicine in Baltimore[1]. Barry argues that this is not a myth. We truly use a very small percentage of our brain. I personally agree that we have yet to scratch the surface of utilizing our mind to its full potential. We have a lot to learn about ourselves.

I remember my college astronomy professor stating that we know more about the universe than we know about earth, the planet we inhabit. This is also true about studying ourselves. We study others so much more than we study our own behavior and our own functionalities, that it's hard for us to purposefully adapt, improve and develop. We start judging, pointing fingers, comparing ourselves to others, and although unintentionally, we spend time doing this, instead of working to harvest our own distinct abilities. The more we do this, the more it will leave us less time to improve our self. This game of comparison, and trying to get better by studying others often backfires and misleads us to the exact opposite of self-discovery and happiness!

"What the eyes see and the ears hear, the mind believes."

~Harry Houdini[2]

The more we compare ourselves to others, the more our mind plays tricks on us, and the more cautious we become about what we see and how we feel. With time, we build our own illusions of reality, as we see the inconsistency in what makes us happy.

So, what can give us hope for good things and success in an uncertain future? And if the future is so uncertain, how can we stay hopeful towards it?

We call that faith, and in many cases, faith simply doesn't "make sense." There is no mathematical equation for it, and science doesn't prove it. But self-control takes faith in God and yourself with lots of practice just like any other skill set. Having one healthy meal doesn't improve your health. Taking one trip to the gym does not produce noticeable results, just as having a single interaction with a peer does not build a friendship. One compli-ment to your spouse doesn't solve the problem, or magically improve your marriage. Rather, it's the faith in the routine that gets you to the successful result that strengthens your faith. The person with the least amount of faith, is the consistent and constant quit-ter, who never sees the results of a faithful, disciplined process.

Think about something you're good at, a skill or quality or talent. Did you develop that ability *without* time, practice and faith?

Odds are, you put a lot of time and effort into it and to do that, you had to get better control of your mind. We are too easily influenced by others, instead of getting better at *in! uencing* ourselves. Whether we like to think of it this way or not, we sell ourselves and our services to others all the time. Perhaps it's as straightforward as selling a product, or selling yourself at an interview; or maybe it's subtler, like convincing others to understand your viewpoint, or to make better decisions, or disagreeing with an opposing viewpoint, or explaining a lesson to your kids. We want to get so good at who we are that we start influencing others' minds so much so, that they see you as a walking example of what they aspire to be. Influence is only easy when you believe and do, it is extremely difficult when you just *tell*.

We all have that one friend, relative, mentor or a colleague that we admire immensely. They're the person who we ask, "what would *they* do?" in a given situation. Yet, despite how much we admire this person, we're often unwilling to make the sacrifices that person made, to be who they are. While I'm very much against living a life to impress others, I am all for living a life that influences and inspires others. When you can do this, you make others better, and more positive.

Of course, it takes a lot of work to inspire other people. First, you have to be the best *you* can be, which requires patience, time, hard work and self-development. There's less work involved in "impressing" others by buying nice clothes, a fancy car and showing a flashy attitude.

Humans are curious beings. We study things like the universe, gravity, anatomy, biology, and religion, but often do so, without asking ourselves what these answers mean to us. Francis Chan one of my favorite preachers once said "Our greatest fear should not be of failure but of succeeding at things in life that don't really matter." Knowing how our minds work, and really finding the answers to questions about ourselves, will bring the answers to questions that matter most. This will lead to a balance of happiness. Being able to understand how our mind works, is the first step towards balance in life. The difference between living a meaningful life for yourself with intention and purpose, and the exact opposite of wasting a life lived for others, all comes down to your mindset, your own thoughts, and your own actions. So, what is the exact balance I talk about that makes you 100% successful?

F4 FORMULA - THE FOUR FACTORS OF TRUE SUCCESS

25% Family + 25% Fitness + 25% Friendship + 25% Finances = 100% Success

The conditions that lead to success never come before the mindset. Achieving true success requires that you fulfill these four factors, not in any specific order, as you can't work on all four at once. However, you can start on the one that needs the most attention first, and prioritize from there.

1. **Family**: I only learned this after I became a husband and a father of my two boys. There is something very special about coming home to your family. Whatever you thought your motivations and inspirations were, after having children, they become your entire purpose of existence. You want to do everything and anything for your family. When it comes to true

happiness and success, this motivating factor is unmatched. I've also learned that to some people family is their pets, their parents, their siblings, relatives, a domestic partner or all of those. Personally for me that stable feeling of *family* came with my wife and kids, which later got me to appreciate my relationship with my parents, brother and sister even more.

2. **Fitness**: It is very important to achieve balance with your health, after all no one wants a weak and stressed out body. You have to be in the right physical and mental state to do right by others. A sound body and a sound mind are parallels, it's almost impossible to sustain one without the other long term. In order to have a healthy mindset a healthy body is a prerequisite.

3. **Friendship**: No matter how much you might have on your plate, and what you are going through, you need a support system to get you through it. Sometimes, nothing beats just hanging out with friends and enjoying their company, over a cup of coffee or a beer.

Finances: Of course, it takes money and power in our current society to have certain luxuries such as buying time for family, food, shelter, fitness and friends. When people say money doesn't buy happiness, it's true, but being a slave to your job does not make you happy. Neither does having debt!

The 14 Principles divided among these four factors, will impart habits that will lead to continuous balanced success.

· · ·

The best part, is that most of what I share can be practiced right away, and easily implemented as part of your daily routine. The good news is, it costs zero dollars to start making a commitment to better habits for a more prosperous life!

Think about the goals you have, and the achievements you want under your belt five years from now. What would have to happen for you to be happy with your results? Only you know the answer. If you don't, now's the time to figure it out.

Start with writing your goals down and making choices that bring you closer to them. It is just as important to eliminate any activity that gets in the way of your daily productivity. I have seen countless people that had no idea what they wanted, simply settled for what came to them. For example: settling for the job you don't like because you are clueless on what you want to do, ending up in a relationship that kind of sort of happened to you as you don't know who you really want to spend the rest of your life with or settling for average health because you have no health goals as you're happy just by not having any major concerns.

Being purposeful is uncomfortable as it requires disruption, which is why people have the tendency to become so comfortable with avoiding purpose that their ambitions towards success die off. If you follow the principles laid out in this book, you can be sure, this won't happen to you. Let me tell you a little about myself, so the Principles make more sense.

· · ·

To access more tools and resources from Hayk, visit: www.haykt.org/mindset-resources

MY STORY

I was born in Armenia, located in the Southern Caucasus Mountains, and the smallest of the former Soviet republics.

Armenia did not have a large economy. It is not known for its prosperity or international influence around the world. Growing up and even today, it is very common for parents to travel back and forth to neighboring countries for trading and business opportunities.

This is the reason why my family moved back and forth between Armenia and Russia multiple times. Moving from country-to-country had long-term effects on my development and personality. I heard many stories from my father about how tough it was in the early 90s, but I was too young to remember. However, the first time I understood what the lack of money meant stands out clearly in my mind.

I was playing outside with my friend David one morning. His family was doing well, which in my neighborhood meant his parents could afford to buy him a brand new bicycle. It was my birthday, so David promised to wake up as early as possible to let me ride his bike as much as I wanted as a birthday gift. I was six years old and having the time of my life riding David's bicycle. A few hours later, my father pulled up in our jalopy of a car, with my mom in the front passenger seat, and my brother and sister in the back. My mom rolled down the window and my father yelled, "Hayk, come get in the car, we are leaving town."

As I went closer to the car my father said, "Give the bike back to David and get in. We are leaving right now." He sounded upset, and I knew better than to talk back to my father, especially when he was upset. I didn't want to be lectured for the entire day. My father was known for his long lectures. I got in the car as I was told, and began crying as we drove away.

Traditional birthday get-togethers in our town were very old school and simple. Parents would cook lots of food, and guests would just show up and bring presents throughout the day. All you had to do was keep the food and drinks coming so the guests were fed, and happy. But my parents told me that we had no money to set a table, so we were going to spend some time at the farmhouse that we inherited from my grandparents after they passed away.

I was very hungry during the car ride, so I asked my mother for food and to this day, I remember the helpless, sad look on her face. She turned around, gave me a piece of hard candy and said, "Eat this till we get to the farmhouse. The neighbor gave us a couple of pieces and all we have for now is just this one candy. I gave the other ones to your brother and sister."

Soon thereafter, my father got a job in Russia, so we all moved there. I was the first dark- haired, brown-skinned kid in school, and I remember kids pointing at me and laughing while saying stuff in Russian that I could not understand, but none of which sounded like good things.

After a few more moves back and forth between Russia and

Armenia, my father came to me one morning and told me that we were leaving again. He said we could only obtain a visa for two so both of us were moving to the United States to pursue the American Dream leaving my mom, sister and brother behind. I was thirteen years old at the time. He explained to me that people could make a good living there because of the stable economy and good government. I didn't know what to say, so I quietly sat back while my dad was selling me the idea of moving to another country again. This time, it was another continent altogether.

When he left the room, I cried for hours. Fortunately, this time we had a few weeks to pack and I had some time to say goodbye to my friends.

We arrived in Los Angeles during the scorching hot summer of 2001. It took us hours just to get past customs, and the person that was supposed to pick us up at the airport never showed up. Luckily, many of the people in Los Angeles spoke Armenian, and we found a cab driver that spoke Armenian.

We got a ride to my father's friend's house, the man who had first moved to the US and encouraged my father to follow. After a few weeks in LA, my father couldn't find any work. My uncle Vartan, from my mother's side, lived in Washington State and invited us to live with him. He told us he would help us find work there. So, once again, we packed up our luggage and got on a bus to Washington.

Going to school was a difficult experience. I was the only kid who did not speak English at my school in Gig Harbor, so the school provided a teacher just for me. She met with me weekly to teach me the basics of English. I often cried in between classes and after school. I tried my best to hide my tears because I was embarrassed.

Finding work was a problem for my father. He had no education, faced a language barrier, and had no connections. We moved from city to city when he found a job with a traveling construction company that moved city to city with each project which had a few Russian speaking people that he became friends with. In two years, I went to four different middle schools, and 3 high schools.

It might sound odd, but I'm very glad I went through what I did. I'm a strong believer that adversity is a huge part of what makes us who we become. It's not the negative experiences themselves, but how you react to being exposed to difficulty. After all, not many people like doing push-ups, but they like feeling strong and healthy. If I hadn't experienced what I did, I wouldn't have the relationships I have now. I wouldn't have the understanding or appreciation of things that people without experience take for granted.

One thing I know for sure, there are no mistakes in our past. It's all an opportunity to improve tomorrow, and become a better person mentally, emotionally and physically.

The weaknesses and fears I faced taught me lessons, which became advantageous in business. I developed a pit bull like bite on financial stability. Hard work and focus became second nature to me. I was so afraid of having to move around for opportunity again, I developed a steel strength work ethic that ensured that I was able to take advantage of opportunities in front of me so I wouldn't have to look for financial stability elsewhere. I became the first person in my family to break a six-figure income, for no other reason than my fear of my past happening again. I developed a strong sense of confidence that my early life experiences had beaten out of me, and grew courage that I had lost somewhere in the past during my unstable childhood. It took some soul searching for me to reflect back on how I developed such courage and confidence and I realized it formed like a muscle through practice. I remember meeting with clients was intimidating and speaking to groups of more than two gave me sweaty palms, red face and often I would lose my train of thought. And forget talking to successful people as they intimidated the life out of me. I really had to work on myself and practice with friends, family and I kept on recording myself just so I could hear how terrible I was with people. A tipping point for me was when I was finally able to switch my mentality from "are they going to like me" to thinking "am I going to like them". I've always had great fear of rejection, and like a muscle I strengthened it but it does not mean the fear is gone I just got better at managing it - as Mark Twain once said "Courage is resistance to fear, mastery of fear, not absence of fear."

I'm not sharing these things for you to feel bad for me. I am sharing these things to let you know you have a choice, to either complain about your past, or let it mold you into the better person that you are today, or want to be.

Now that you know a little more about me, you might be better able to relate to my interpretation of what balanced success is, and how our daily habits can help us achieve true success and happiness. I want to show you the steps to knowingly control your mind. Too many people, myself included, allow themselves to be controlled by their environment. They *let* things happen, instead of *making* things happen. Balance is easily attainable. The reason it escapes many of us is because we judge our success based on others. It becomes extremely difficult to achieve balance and success when we chase something that doesn't exist, and take our eyes off our own happiness.

The 14 Principles will break down the tools and easy to implement steps, to having better self-control. This in turn will allow you to attain a perfect balance with your life in terms of what matters most *to you*.

Most humans are very emotional beings. Michael Levine[1] a publicist, motivational speaker and author of 19 books published an article on Psychology Today on July 12th, 2012 called *Logic and Emotion* where he talks about 80% of our choices are emotional and only 20% are logical. Which totally made sense as I catch myself making emotional choices all the time.

I agree with that percentage and I often feel as though I'm making an emotional decision, 100% of the time. It all depends on the state of mind or vibration level you're in at any given moment. You rarely attract what you *want*; you usually attract what you *are*. Making decisions when you're in a highly emotional state is almost always a bad idea.

So how does one develop the necessary habits for self-control? The first step is to make sure you understand you likely have poor self-control, which no longer makes it a blind spot.

The second step, just like any other skill-set, is practice and routine. To master anything takes 10,000 hours of practice --a concept first introduced in a 1993 paper written by Anders Erics-son, a Professor at the University of Colorado, called *The Role of Deliberate Practice in the Acquisition of Expert Performance*[2].

Ericsson explained that the practice has to be "deliberate," or the concept of, "perfect practice makes it perfect." That means, you can't become an expert at something while practicing poorly for 10,000 hours. Learning a new trade, a new language, a new sport, or a new business takes 10,000 deliberate hours to master. But some of the smaller things like committing to a morning workout, improving a marriage, or improving a business can happen with a simple instant commitment.

Understanding the 14 Principles, I was able to obtain a strong and comfortable level of mindset and become purposeful and motivated towards balanced success. I have observed, surrounded myself with, and studied many physically, emotionally, socially, and financially successful people. I also know plenty of multi-millionaires, professional athletes, fitness icons, and social butterflies whom I do not consider successful, as they have not figured out the proper balance of success. Although, I will never put down anyone's great achievements because I know how much work it can take to be great at something. I will question whether that person is successfully balanced, or is merely obsessed with a small part of success. Those who sacrifice other factors of success to maintain what they believe success to be.

To access more tools and resources from Hayk, visit: www.haykt. org/mindset-resources

CHAPTER ONE
SELF-FULFILLMENT USING THE F4 FORMULA

Goals of This Chapter:

- Understand the most important concept in this book: *your mindset comes before your conditions*
- Understand the source of lasting happiness and change
- Become aware of *who* is determining your desired conditions
- Define success and understand how to use the F^4 Formula to achieve it
- Learn how to develop the habit of getting comfortable with the uncomfortable
- Discover the missing link between success and comfort

YOUR MINDSET COMES BEFORE YOUR CONDITIONS

Imagine a happy family: two parents, two kids, a dog and a cat living in a nice neighborhood, with a perfectly groomed yard, white picket fence, with expensive cars parked in the driveway. You might assume that this picturesque scene would make you happy, but what you may not know, is that this couple was happy *before* this scene, before they acquired the nice house, the cars, gave birth to the kids and adopted the pets.

You may believe you need to have certain needs and conditions met to be happy but this is not true. You don't need the picket fence, or the luxury car, or the large bank account, to be happy. However, as humans, we have a tendency to base our happiness on others' conditions and parameters.

Let's use social media as an example. Women look at fitness models, new moms look at other moms, who make it all look so easy. Professionals look at successful businessmen, and women posting pictures of their private jets and exotic cars. Of course, a lot of what people post online is exaggerated, but even knowing this, it's important to understand the way someone is, or the way someone looks, is mainly the outcome of their mindset.

As you believe, so you become. We don't need someone else's condition to be happy. Our conditions are the outcomes of our minds.

Happy people achieve certain things because they were happy to begin with. As such, the key to success in life -- and we'll define what success means in a moment -- is cultivating a healthy positive mindset *right now*, wherever you are in life, whether you are poor or already rich. Whether you are happily single or happily married. Only then, can you start to make the right decisions and take the actions required to create the new conditions you desire.

WHEN YOU NEED NOTHING, YOU CAN ACT COURAGEOUSLY - THE ILLUSION OF NEED

Let's address something I call the Illusion of Need. When you can differentiate your needs from your wants, you can strengthen your mindset substantially. When we focus primarily on what we *want*, we let our environment control us. We rarely think for ourselves, and instead live for others' opinions. But when we focus on what we need, we no longer let others influence our decisions - or our lives.

It's pretty simple to differentiate a want from a need. Try holding your breath for as long as you can. You NEED to breathe to live. You don't need that new pair of shoes, or the next generation iPhone. Most of us live in a world of wants. We are so caught up in competing against others that we develop an illusion of need that does not exist. Imagine you were submerged under water. The only thing you would think about is being able to breathe. In that moment, you definitely *need* air. However, most people rarely find themselves in this kind of life or death situation. Most of the time we have no needs. *Most of things people claim to need aren't truly needs at all* -- unless one is gasping for air, starving, sick or malnourished.

Have you ever noticed that when you make more money, you don't necessarily save more? Odds are, you're spending more on wants, your desire to obtain what you think you are missing. In our tendency to think we will always need the next thing, we get stressed and weak, playing a game we can't win. In many ways, we start lacking the courage to take control of our own lives.

Let's assume that survival and safety is guaranteed a majority of the time, for most of us -- which is pretty close to our daily given odds. When we can abstain from stressing about all the different things/conditions we "need" (that we don't), we start developing very powerful, positive and courageous thoughts towards the future. Those thoughts turn into actions, actions lead to activity, and activity leads to positive results. It is very crucial to understand how important it is to be courageous and the importance of courage. Courage has a lot to do with being present. Often, thoughts of the future usually lead to reminders of our fears, while thinking about our past leads to thinking of regret.

The next time you catch yourself either in future fear, or past regret, stop and start counting your blessings. I promise you that will make you present and courageous right away.

Both the past and the future negatively impact our courage. They turn us into creatures of safety, which prevents us from the necessary, actionable steps success requires. Whether it's going for that job interview, asking that person out on a date, buying a gym membership, apologizing, or forgiving etc., fear and regret will kill your action towards good risk. The only real risk in life is not taking risks at all.

When we aren't focused on fulfilling our wants, we can grow more confident, because we are less distracted by our desire for more material things. Less distraction means more focus, and more focus means more deliberate practice towards our actual needs, versus spending most of our lives in fearful distraction, chasing what we believe success to be.

So instead of worrying about being more courageous, focus more on being present. Practicing presence will help build courage, which is a huge asset during times of risk and difficult decision-making - especially targeted towards true needs associated with our family, health, friends and money.

CULTIVATE A HEALTHY MINDSET TO BUILD A STRONG FOUNDATION

Wealth is built over time and (usually) cannot be taken away easily. Of course, some people can inherit or stumble upon riches without realizing, or appreciating what they have. In those cases, it can be taken away as quickly as it was acquired.

Of course there are exceptional people in all cases, but I'm talking about on a global scale. No one ever built a vast amount of wealth from zero to where they are now in a short period of time and without hard work. It always takes time, and hustle.

Wealth is not necessarily a reflection of one's financial status. My definition of wealth is the long-term acquisition of balance in family, fitness, finances and friendship - acquiring those things in the order that relates to what you lack most at the moment. So if you are lacking health for example, you should make health your main focus of your total success journey. You must build a foundation first and ensure that it's able to carry a substantial amount of weight. This foundation may include a supportive family, good health, large business or a good group of friends.

CREATING A NEW MINDSET GUARANTEES LASTING CHANGE

I have seen people with eating disorders lose weight and gain it right back. I have seen some starve, take unhealthy supplements and even resort to surgeries -- often just to gain the weight again. The ones that gain the weight back are the ones who placed the desired result first, instead of conditioning a new mindset.

If one assumes a skinny body will bring happiness, he or she may use intense methods to get quick results, but neglect to allow time for their mind to adapt. They never ask themselves what led to the initial, undesirable results in the first place, and instead of working backward, they look for shortcuts. While they may end up appearing differently, they feel exactly the same way they did before. They often return to their old habits and are right back where they began. I've seen women resort to unhealthy starving diets just to quickly attain the skinny look and over time gain the weight back. Or men result to steroids to gain muscle but end up depressed when their doctor tells them they need to get off the drug and lose all their gains. Although there are people with serious health concerns who need a lot more than a mindset change to be healthy, in most cases, when you do things the healthy way, it's hard to have bad results.

WHO IS DECIDING WHAT YOUR DREAM LIFE LOOKS LIKE?

Before we dive into the F^4 formula, I want to make sure you understand how important your mindset is to truly being able to implement the success formula.

Social media like Facebook, Instagram, Twitter, and even Snapchat, show a side of people that you rarely see in person, because it is the life they've created on social media for others to see. For people who feel sad or insecure in their own lives, seeing this can feel frustrating. But often, the people who seem most successful and happy online, are also struggling. We can write anything we want on the internet. It's the "bathroom wall," of our society. But it's often an illusion of perfection from the insecurities people have of themselves.

Often, after I become friends with those who I meet on social media. It's ironic, because I've noticed people are very different on the internet versus what my perception was when I met them in person.

Not everyone, but in this specific group I'm talking about, people tend to post pictures of their designer clothes, trips they take several times per year, businesses they are considering purchasing, mountains they want to climb, the nice new Bentley they just bought by trading in their three-year-old Maserati, and their check-ins at expensive restaurants. Most people don't live such lavish lifestyles, don't take nearly as many vacations, and don't wear designer brands. Again, there are exceptional people who truly find joy with these things as these are merely conditions of their mindset but these are rare successful individuals. Certain hard working and very successful people I know personally love the nicer things in life and props to them. Most others compare themselves to these individuals thinking copying their conditions will bring them their mindsets – unfortunately it never does. The disconnect here is that successful peoples lifestyle, standard of living, trips, clothes, material are all a result of who they are, a result of their mindset which later brought their conditions. To merely have their lifestyle will not bring satisfaction, but to start having their mindset which is often the harder route as it requires discipline, hard work, dedication, perseverance, integrity etc. is the real target you should seek. When you observe people who put conditions before the mindset you will see a consistent pattern of struggle in their life between the balance of true wealth, health and having good relationships. Watching people in this group brag about their lifestyle can demotivate you, making you feel disap-pointed about your accomplishments so be careful   when comparing yourself to them.

We are in an era of consuming information through our smart-phones, and a computer screen. Who we falsely admire, can be very deceptive and demotivating at times. So it's crucial to under-stand what true success is, versus someone else's poorly expressed insecurities, before we start thinking about what we want out of our life.

I've caught myself doing this before. However, I ultimately realized that people boast like this because it satisfies their addiction to temporary feelings of happiness. I know a lot of people that are part of this group, as I too have been part of this group, I know exactly what's going on.

They don't make as much as they show to others, and they have more credit card debt in their thirties than I will ever have in my lifetime. But of course flaws are not disclosed, as some people only show perfection on the surface. So you need to ask yourself how well you know the source that you admire. They may not be *really* happy -- so they create a virtual life of perfection to make up for it.

Consider whether you may be admiring the wrong people, for the wrong reasons. Your purpose of living needs to be *your* best, -- not better than a fake image of a virtual person, or people in your community that do nothing but flatter themselves around you. So, ask yourself whether you are living your life, or living to a standard of life, set by images of others, that do not exist.

Now I want to introduce you to my F^4 formula. I use my F^4 formula to bring more awareness in my life, and to balance out my success, in all areas that matter the most to me. This formula will help you maintain a success level that feels natural, and allows you to focus on what matters, in the right order.

To access more tools and resources from Hayk, visit: www.haykt. org/mindset-resources

THE F4 FORMULA FOR SUCCESS: FILLING THE 4 TANKS

Let's make sure we're on the same page when it comes to the definition of success. To me, success means that contentment only comes when all of your needs are being met in four key areas simultaneously: Family, Fitness, Friendship and Finances. If you aren't addressing your needs in all four of these areas or pillars, then eventually one pillar will come crashing down, taking the other pillars down with it.

Equally important to note is that it is impossible to fill all four tanks simultaneously. You build one pillar at a time starting from the one you lack the most, first. Although these pillars are something we all want in life, now is the perfect time to restructure your understanding of needs, and put these pillars, into the same category, as a need.

Do you want to have a successful and purposeful life? Then you absolutely need to balance out these four pillars. Make sure these pillars are not in the same need category as a new pair of shoes or a new car. Those things only bring temporary excitement which fade away just as fast as they came. When you know what you need to be successful, and you put them in the need category, you will find a way. The first and most important step is clarity.

Clarity will lead to action, action will lead to activity and activity will lead to results.

Even if you have a ton of money, you could be out of shape. You can be a professional athlete with no time for anything else outside of training and an intense diet. You can be a great parent to a large family with no money to support them. Or, you can be a social butterfly with tons of friends, but nothing else serious outside of hanging out and socializing. If one tank is full, but the others are near zero, you're likely to be an unhappy and unsuccessful individual.

I know this because I've been there. I've been extremely wealth-focused, but had no life outside of work. I've been extremely health-focused, but broke. I've been extremely social, but not family oriented. I've gotten so involved in family time, that I neglected my health and ambition in business.

By sharing my own mistakes and how I overcame them, I hope to bring you a process whereby you can balance these four pillars. I think it's very appropriate to throw in one of my favorite quotes from Albert Einstein,

> Dumb people don't learn anything, smart people learn from their mistakes and geniuses learn from others' mistakes.

We don't live nearly long enough to learn all the lessons mistakes teach us. So, learning from others is crucial, and is a very easy way to become a genius.

To access more tools and resources from Hayk, visit: www.haykt. org/mindset-resources

(F4) FORMULA

FAMILY, FITNESS, FRIENDSHIP, FINANCES

25%/25%/25%/25%
100% Success

It doesn't matter what order you add twenty-five four times, the result will always be 100. Although the formula has Family as 1st, Fitness 2nd, Friendship 3rd and Finances 4th, one is not necessarily more important than the other; remember, the idea is to achieve balance.

Everyone achieves their 100% differently. Every tank gets filled unique to the person's life, at various times. Mine started with my financial tank, which is what I'll dive into first. There is no right answer, to where to start. Only when the 100% is achieved, will you know how to balance the formula for continuous fulfillment. The following story of my own experience will help you understand where you are.

To access more tools and resources from Hayk, visit: www.haykt. org/mindset-resources

MY 1ST F- FINANCES

FILLING MY FINANCIAL TANK

As I discussed in the book's introduction, I grew up poor - so I believed that money was the missing ingredient in my life, the thing that would make me comfortable. I noticed cars we could not afford to drive, homes we could not afford to live in, restaurants where we could not afford to eat.

Speaking of restaurants, I had never been to a restaurant until we moved to United States when I was 13 years old.

A friend's family invited me to a local pizzeria. I remember not knowing what to do when I was given a glass to get myself a beverage. Not being able to speak English didn't help, I didn't want anyone to know this was my first time in a restaurant of any kind. I was ashamed, but I managed to survive and worked up the courage to visit the all-you-can-eat pizza table. I ate that pizza like it was the finest filet mignon in the world.

Throughout the first couple of years living in America, my father and I rented rooms from others until we were approved for low-income housing. We visited food banks, borrowed money to pay rent - and even went without food from time to time. This led to a large hole in my heart that I *thought* could only be filled with money. I was so uncomfortable with being poor, that I naturally thought the opposite would make me comfortable.

Growing up, I prepared myself for any financial opportunity with so much focus, that I was ready to do anything, to succeed. I made commitments to multiple businesses which included multi-level marketing, flipping foreclosed homes, taking on construction projects, selling insurance, selling financial products, and franchise consulting. I found a way - several ways, in fact, to make the money, I'd always been seeking. Yet, no matter how much financial "success" I achieved, I still felt unfulfilled.

By then, I was beginning to understand, success wasn't really about the money. (although I wasn't *complaining* about having a continuous-growing financial freedom and the option to stop working full time in my mid-20s, with a very comfortable multi-six figure and growing residual income.) Yet I still felt unsuccessful, by my own definition I simply wasn't happy. I was starting to understand the missing link between success, and comfort.

I began to recognize what I was missing. I was growing wiser through my experiences -- or as my mentor Ali likes to call it, "cautiously optimistic." I noticed that when I got excited about something I didn't attain, I would be incredibly - even excessively - let down. If I was 100% excited about something, and things didn't go as planned, I wouldn't just get down to 0% -- I would get to -100% disappointed. It was not a good place to be mentally. It would take me way too long to recover from -100, versus hovering around 0 where I started. But the more lessons I endured, the more I learned how to be *cautiously* optimistic. In other words, I learned to hover around 0.

I was beginning to learn that control is an illusion, and there are very few things I can control in life. I have a lot of faith in God, and I am not a in any way qualified to predict my future. All I can control is to give my best today, and if the results are not desired, then it's for the best. Failure often brings us better lessons than winning does! Here is an illustration of how I see *cautious optimism*.

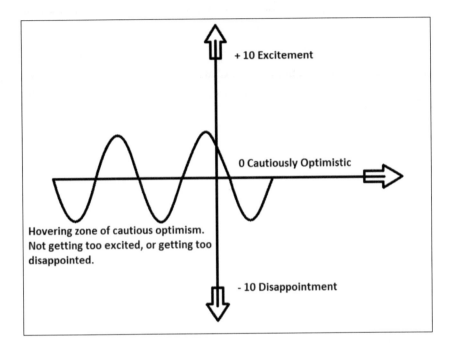

It goes without saying, emotions are hard to control. But the more I got to know financially successful people, the more I noticed how and why, they were so well composed, and had such a calm demeanor. It takes time and daily improvement to reach this level of wisdom. People who don't or can't are likely not learning from their experiences. Most of us make our best decisions when we are thinking logically, and considering facts without too much excitement or disappointment. That's when I learned filling my financial tank is not the only driver to my happiness. Of course, lack of money doesn't make you happy either, but obtaining what I've always wanted, didn't get me the feeling I was looking for. So I became more self-aware about my goals. I learned that we want what we lack most, which is often emotional security from our past experiences. When we work really hard to obtain what we are lacking, we have to pay attention to the cost of getting there.

For me, I sacrificed my health to achieve my financial goals, and looking back, the sacrifice was not necessary. I could have easily maintained both. *An ounce of prevention is worth a pound of cure.* But figuring out finances is extremely important, as it buys you time, and with time, you can work on the other tanks with a lot more efficiency.

To access more tools and resources from Hayk, visit: www.haykt. org/mindset-resources

MY 2ND F-FITNESS

FILLING MY FITNESS & HEALTH TANK

Over time, I began to understand that financial success wouldn't make me fully comfortable. I had taken a lot of time away from an important part of my life: my health. So I turned my focus to getting back into good physical shape. I started to take fitness breaks at 3:00 PM every day, and told my team not to call me unless there was an emergency. As time went on, I noticed positive changes in my business. I started to realize that I was handicapping my team by always being in the office. With me leaving for a little while every day, I was giving them ownership, and an opportunity to become better, independent decision makers.

I observed a dramatic increase in the mood and performance from the good team members, and a decline in the ones I was already considering letting go. I ended up getting rid of the bad employees, and the good ones became great. Although I physically spent less time in the office, our production numbers started increasing. My team got smaller, but I had only winners now, so my expenses were less. This resulted in growing my net income.

This was the complete opposite of what I initially thought would take place when I began leaving the office to work out. I began to trust my team even more -- and they sensed and appreciated that.

Business improvement was just one part of the positive change when I incorporated more fitness into my days. I noticed dramatic results after it became a habit, within a month. I also noticed a positive increase in my mood, higher energy levels and a more optimistic approach to my day. Sometimes it would be 12:00PM to 3:00PM or 3:00PM to 6:00PM. That time was reserved as my "alone time" five days per week. My best ideas came to me during that time.

Back when I was focused solely on work, I told myself that I needed my energy for the business whirlwind -- and would only drain that energy. When I first began to work out, I was still mentally connected to the business. I kept thinking about all the tasks I was taking time away from - which of course just stressed me out even more.

My average day consisted of putting out fires, cold-calling for several hours, payroll, production, money tracking, team training, joint and personal appointments, negotiations, agreement reviews, pre-underwriting, dealing with vendors, writing and replying to hundreds of emails, working with human resources on employee-related drama, hiring/firing, expense tracking - and countless other office and people related issues I could think of. It took some practice to block out all those "to-do's", and to be away from the office physically and mentally. But once I let go of the false belief that I needed to use ALL my energy on work, the exact opposite happened.

After the first month, I was more energized than ever before. It was a complete paradox. I was getting into peak physical shape, at the same time as my business was growing. My team started asking me questions about what I was doing and started their own workout programs.

My colleagues kept hearing my marathon prep stories, seeing

my noticeable muscle gain and listening to some *occasional* bragging of how fast I could run. (I never thought I could beat my high school one mile time of 5:15 --- but now I could do a mile in five minutes flat, and I was pretty proud of that!).

Soon, I also stopped working weekends and instead went to train MMA with my brother on Sundays after church. I had a noticeable pep in my step. The new schedule worked really well. I figured out a great work and fitness balance. I was in peak shape, and money was good.

Yet, I was still feeling unfulfilled. I had filled both financial and fitness tanks to the top -- but felt far from *fulfilled*. I asked myself, "What in the world am I missing? I don't have time to add anything more. I have everything I've ever wanted, and I'm doing all I can."

Of course, I was wrong. It wasn't that I wasn't doing *enough*, it was because I was not allocating my time and effort *correctly*. I doubt anyone gets their time management perfect, and I was no exception. I was still learning -- but most importantly, I was open to change what I needed versus being close-minded and thinking I had it all figured out. After all,

"a mind is like a parachute: it only works when it's open" - Anthony D'Angelo

To access more tools and resources from Hayk, visit: www.haykt. org/mindset-resources

MY 3RD F- FRIENDSHIP

THE LONELY EXOTIC CAR GUY FILLS HIS
FRIENDSHIP TANK

It took some digging for me to realize I was missing something very important. With all my time going towards fitness and finances, I had no time left for friends. Yet again, I recognized the blind spot, and put my focus towards another part of my life- my friends. I have no idea how I allowed this to slip away. Friends always brought so much value and happiness into my life. I guess the saying "it worked so well we stopped doing it," can be applied even towards very vital parts of our lives, such as friendship.

I unintentionally started to ignore my friends, and was beginning to become what I was afraid of becoming: the lonely Exotic car guy, a wealthy young punk with no friends who has to surround himself with nice toys to get the attention that he's lacking. Although I didn't actually *own* an exotic car, I had gotten something just as fast, for the same reason -- attention. I use this metaphor because I have seen countless people who have issues of being accepted -- either by the opposite sex or by a group they admire - so they buy a fancy car.

However, it does nothing but grant temporary gratification. When I approached my real friends, they confirmed what I had suspected. They felt my success had gone to my head, and that I now thought I was too good to hang out with them.

The invites to fancy parties and the attention I was getting in the corporate world had gotten to me. Plenty of people go through this -- but few realize its downsides. I definitely enjoyed the public recognition, countless emails with publicity articles that had my name at the top. I enjoyed people coming up to me at meetings to tell me they heard about me, and wanted to invite me to lunch or dinner, or to speak at their events. It was all great - until it wasn't. There's a point when you realize, fame and success brings you fun -- but only temporarily. This was when I learned the difference between fun, and happy. I realized that I needed to stop pursuing the attention of others, and start spending quality time with quality people. My true friends were watching and waiting on me to call.

Once I realized what I'd done, I made some changes. I started leaving the office earlier, taking early/late lunch breaks with friends, and spending the weekends with my friends. I sold my fancy car and learned in the process how bad of a money pit it was (for those wondering it was a V10 BMW M5 with every perfor- mance modification you can think of). I lost fifty thousand dollars in its depreciation, modifications and maintenance costs, which I could have invested into a rental property. At the rate real estate had boomed in Seattle Washington, the property would have doubled its value in five years.

Talking about learning a huge lesson, I also started spending my money more modestly, and became conscious of my image in the community. The right people appreciated the changes I made and stuck around, the ones that disappeared during my transition weren't true friends to begin with. That famous 80/20 rule applied here. I was now spending 80% of my time with the 20% of people who mattered the most. By eliminating 80% of my acquaintances, I created plenty of time to be with my 20%, of good friends. Those were the ones who didn't need to go somewhere fancy for dinner or drinks, didn't wear the latest fashion to fit in, didn't get offended when I offered to get tacos from a food truck for lunch, didn't care what car I drove, and most of all, who made me feel as though they'd be there for me, no matter the circumstance.

To access more tools and resources from Hayk, visit: www.haykt. org/mindset-resources

MY 4TH F- FAMILY

CREATING MY FAMILY TANK

At this point, I had three of my life tanks full. I had to tone down my vigorous training program and train less, as I had already obtained the physical shape I was happy with. I was happy with now maintaining my health.

I missed a few award-winning performance bonuses in business - but I was okay with that, as I didn't get into business for plaques. I got into business for financial freedom and to create jobs in the community. I was a good friend, good businessman and in very good physical shape. But I still felt I was missing something, and this time it felt like something *big*. One part of me wondered if I was expecting too much from myself, but another part felt the drive to find out what I was lacking, as soon as possible.

Being part of an Armenian family - a culture where arranged marriages are still practiced, -- I felt a lot of pressure from my family to get married. So I stopped avoiding relationships as I believed to be too busy for one at the time, and started looking for that special person to commit to.

I was adamantly against an arranged marriage. It was completely out of the question for me as I enjoyed the process of getting to know someone too much and I was too Americanized to follow my old Armenian tradition. I learned that being good with people, and having a relationship-building business wasn't just good for business, it was also helpful getting the attention of the women I wanted to pursue.

One morning I got a message from a Facebook friend that she needed to get insurance. A few mutual friends had recommended my agency to her. Although I usually delegated new clients to my team, I knew she had a roommate named Diana, who was also coming with her, that I found extremely attractive. I moved things around on my calendar, made sure I was available to take the appointment -- and got ready to sell a lot more than just insurance.

The day they came into the office, I did my best to extend myself, and offered to buy them coffee at Starbucks, right after our meeting. The girls were really nice and they accepted my offer.

After getting them Starbucks, and saying our goodbyes, I kept in touch with Diana through social media. One day I finally gathered enough courage to ask for her number, which led to our first date. I have to admit, that was the most amount of sales tactics I had to implement, to get her out on our first date. This was the sales tactic my good friend and mentor Dan shared with me "no is not a rejection, so unless you get rejected you keep on following up". Several times I felt like a stalker as she ignored me or didn't respond to my messages. But being in a sales business where I have to persuade people all day long, I learned not to give up easily.

At the time, I had a wrapped business car with my credentials and picture on both sides. So I picked her up in the business car, for our first date, for the hell of it. I remember her making fun of me for picking her up in a car with a large picture of my face on the doors. The way she did it was so funny that we both had a lot of good laughs as we ate dinner.

She was honest when she told me that she had seen my car,

with my face on it around town, and thought I was really full of myself, and silly. She admitted making fun of me with her friends. Honestly, I was happy that I didn't waste money wrapping a car, since the marketing was working well, and people were noticing. In the beginning phase of my business, I put myself out there and have counseled others to do the same. So if the girl of my dreams noticed, imagine the thousands of others talking about it. I was happy she noticed!

We started dating regularly. Eventually, she met my family who fell in love with her. The dating got better and better until one day, I woke up with a gut feeling knowing I wanted to spend the rest of my life with her. I drove to a jewelry store that morning, bought a ring without any plan, and just kept it in my suit pocket for days. I'm a huge believer in not making commitments when happy or decisions when angry with the understanding that emotional decision making can be catastrophic, so I waited.

About a week after buying the ring, I felt exactly the same about proposing to Diana and that's when I knew my decision was final. We had tickets to a Michael Buble concert that month, so I figured that would be the perfect place to propose. It was the most nervous day of my life.

I sat next to Diana with sweaty palms, and shaky knees. When Buble started singing a song, that felt perfect, I pulled the ring out of my pocket looked at her, but she looked back at me, confused. The ironic part about the song is I was so nervous I couldn't remember which song it was, when I later asked Diana she laughed and told me it was a song called *Everything*. Unfortunately there was no room for me to get on my knee as we were crammed between seats in front and people next to us, so I just looked at her from my seat, filled up my lungs with way too much air for a short question and asked her the most important question we get to ask our entire lives.

"Will you marry me?"

Luckily, she said, "YES."

Diana is now my wife and a wonderful mother to our two boys, David and Arman. My perspective of how things work together has been completely changed. I'm usually out of the house by 6AM while the family is asleep so I can get a workout in before getting into the office. This is coming from a person that claimed that he'd never be a morning person. I even used to make fun of morning people. You have to be careful who you make fun of, as you might join them one day.

It has become a tradition for my wife to send me pictures of our two boys each morning, since I don't see them on the way out. It's interesting how over time, life has a way of completely changing the way we view things. I used to be motivated by exotic cars and mansions, now it's pictures of my family and small things like, squeezing in a short workout during the busier weeks, getting a babysitter and taking my wife out on a date, grabbing a coffee with a friend, working on this book at a coffee shop, watching cartoons with my boys, or tossing a ball around with them.

My comfort zone has completely changed. I have more responsibilities as a father than I ever did as a businessman, athlete, or friend. But somehow, I now get more done on a daily basis and I feel more accomplished. I sleep as much as my body needs, which is around six - seven hours, instead of how much I *want* (which used to be too much!).

Since my time at work is limited, I focus on getting high priority items completed, versus goofing off the way I used to when I had a 12-hour shift to kill. I learned to block all other thoughts I had in my mind during my morning runs, and enjoy a good podcast, audiobooks, or sometimes just listen to music and spend time with myself. I find ways to be productive when I have a free moment, so that I'm not wasting time. Relaxing with family feels much more rewarding after a busy day.

I finally began to understand that the 25%-Family, 25%-Fitness, 25%-Finances, 25%-Friendship scale, is the perfect balance. These elements come in a different order for different people, but they should balance. When I start to spend too much time on one pillar, things get uncomfortable, especially if I don't focus on re-balancing the scale as soon as possible. It's okay to be temporarily unbalanced, as long as you're focused on bringing things back to 25/25/25/25, as soon as possible.

The F^4 Formula helps me understand what I need to get comfortable, and work on to become my version of successful. At this point in my life, the F^4 formula is in full force, and I've never felt happier.

To access more tools and resources from Hayk, visit: www.haykt. org/mindset-resources

GET COMFORTABLE WITH
THE UNCOMFORTABLE

In order to use the advice I share, you need to get comfortable with being uncomfortable. Even the thought of discomfort is very uncomfortable to think about. The idea of not being in a place of peace, or a stable state of mind, is almost dreadful. My notion of "uncomfortable" includes being on a wet couch, with an itchy cover, covered in dirt that I have to sit on with clean clothes. It's important to get comfortable with the uncomfortable.

We all have desires that fall into the four categories - family, fitness, friendship and finances. We decide whether we want to attain or improve these things. It is what drives us and gives us purpose in life. People who have accomplished what you are looking to achieve, likely pushed through and moved forward, during times of discomfort.

If we want what we have never had, we have to do what we have never done. Most new things are uncomfortable, which is why we don't do them. Learning something new, taking risks, allowing for trial and error, and being okay with failure, are all uncomfortable by nature. Yet, they are also prerequisites to success.

My advice on discomfort, especially discomfort towards a good decision, is if it hurts then you need to do more of it. The pain won't necessarily go away, but you will get more tolerant and build up calluses in the right places. Pain is a teacher, so lean towards it, not away.

WHY CHANGE IS SO DIFFICULT

If your current processes have gotten you to what you have, and where you are, and how you are, then what is the first step to making all of those things different? How do you work your way towards what you have never had?

Change involves getting out of your comfort zone. The actual execution of a process for which change is required, is the hardest thing for a human to undertake. Have you ever wondered why so many people quit smoking, but soon revert back to smoking again? That's because the maintenance part of the change is not continued for a long enough time to overcome the addiction. Research has found that change rarely happens in a linear sequence. When we alter our habits that lead to the chain, it's very difficult to go back to how we were before the change.

Writer Brett Steenbarger wrote in *Forbes* magazine about the patterns of people who quit smoking.

He wrote,

> "*Research on the transtheoretical model of change, which emphasizes maintenance as an essential step in the change process, ! nds that people who stop smoking for a full year still have a greater than 40% rate of returning to active smoking. It isn't until ! ve years of abstinence is achieved, that the relapse rate drops below 10%.*"[1]

My father smoked at least a pack of cigarettes per day. I lost count on the amount of times he temporarily quit smoking. The difficult part for him was not making the decision, it was the execution of that decision, and maintenance. The discomfort level associated with withdrawals for those who are addicted, can be incredibly difficult to overcome.

Another interesting article on smokers published in March, 2012 by James O. Prochaska a Professor of Psychology - Harvard Medical School titled, *"Why behavior change is hard - and why you should keep trying"*.[2]

The article included research done on 6,500 middle-aged and elderly smokers over a 20-year period. It explained that:

> *"Those who smoked, were obese or physically inactive, or had diabetes or uncontrolled high blood pressure when the study began, were much more likely to require admission to a nursing home later on. Middle-age smoking increased the chance of a nursing home admission by 56%, physical inactivity by 40%, and uncontrolled high blood pressure by 35%. Diabetes more than tripled the risk. Middle-age obesity was also associated with higher risk, but the association wasn't statistically signi! cant — that is, the numbers could have resulted from chance. All of these conditions can, of course, be modi! ed with lifestyle changes."*

The article goes on to describe how we knowingly continue to do things that are bad for us, even deadly, but treat change as an excuse for procrastination. Change is a process, not a one-time event. The hardest part is to keep the change consistent.

We all build and reside in a mental comfort zone or bubble. We have everything exactly where we want it, and we get so used to how things are set up, that change becomes something to avoid.

No growth, development, improvement, progress or achievement ever comes out of being in your comfort zone. Our brains are wired to keep us safe and avoid all possible change, so it disguises change as danger. We have been wired to seek safety for thousands of years as our lives depended on not taking risks back when wild animals hunted us down while we lived in forests. Shelter and safety is fairly new to us as humans, so imagine thousands of years' worth of genetics are telling us to be safe, not take risks, not to grow, avoid possible failure, ignore potential progress and seek safety in a shelter. All those survival instincts worked in our favor when we were fighting for survival but this same wiring we are born with is working against us in our modern day society. This is why we biologically crave comfort and consistency. It feels safe to us. But today feeling uncomfortable means you are on the right track. You're growing or learning or improving, as unnatural as it can feel. So keep in mind that feeling of discomfort is exactly what you are looking for because it means you're moving forward toward your goals.

To access more tools and resources from Hayk, visit: www.haykt. org/mindset-resources

THE 4 PHASES OF CHANGE

CONTEMPLATION PHASE, IMPLEMENTATION PHASE, EXPERIMENTAL PHASE AND HABIT ESTABLISHMENT PHASE.

PHASE 1. THE CONTEMPLATION PHASE

Every change begins with a thought, and it's always the same thought. Should I commit to this change or not? That's when we recognize we need something to fulfill one or more of our four F's. After a little bit of back and forth, you'll come to a clear understanding that the change is good, and you need to take action towards it.

All healthy changes have steps, just like a staircase. When you start a change and take the first step, you think to yourself, "Okay, that wasn't so bad." Then, you take the second step and realize, okay, wow it was little more work than I thought. Then you take the third step, and realize it's getting tougher or harder. By the time you are on the eighth step, you hate the pain and the discomfort, and think it will continue getting more difficult, and quit. If the tenth step was the tipping point, you just needed two more steps, here is an illustration of what that looks like.

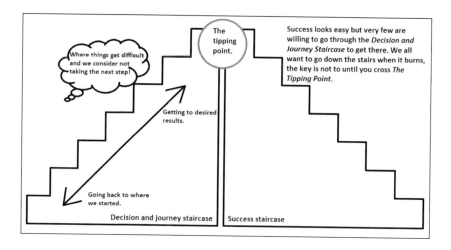

The problem with giving up is it becomes a habit, and results in us giving up when we are very close to victory. The high pain level is usually an indicator of the tipping point being very close to where things get better and easier. But what do we do when things get really tough?

We give up.

The key is when things consistently get tougher, we need to keep in mind that the difficulty of that consistency will eventually decline by the tipping point, and the results will increase and compound, while the required effort will go down. But, you have to be patient.

THIS IS YOUR BRAIN ON AUTOPILOT

Our brain is a very powerful organ. It never rests, and is always gathering information (even while we sleep.) It's constantly healing your body, providing energy, while developing and improving your body. So naturally, because it's so busy, your brain tries to put whatever it can on autopilot. Certain daily habits and routines become what we call "second nature," things we repeat so many times, that they just happen effortlessly which leaves our brains to focus on more important things. These include dealing with negative thoughts, healing your body, gathering information to help prevent illness, and helping you become a better person. Therefore, it's in our brains' best interest to avoid change, since change requires effort and disrupts our "autopilot" mode. In other words, change disturbs our brain's inherent "efficiency," at least for a little while.

But as we know, the more we exercise, the stronger our body gets. If we can move out of the contemplation phase and into the implementation phase, we can give our mind that same kind of exercise, and in turn, make it stronger and more adaptive to good change.

PHASE 2. THE IMPLEMENTATION

Getting comfortable with being uncomfortable doesn't mean that we need to change everything and anything, all at once. It means making small changes and tweaks until we attain a noticeable result. This continuous tweaking is important during Phase 2, the Implementation Phase, as well as in Phase 3, the Experimental Phase, which is where we concentrate on finding what works best.

The Implementation phase is based on our actual actions. For example, let's say you want to get in better shape and decide to, "work out more." That's a pretty ambiguous plan. A clearer, more actionable step might be to say, "I'll spend 30 minutes on the treadmill, ten minutes on the elliptical and do 20 push-ups after." Our mind will get a better grasp of a specific order, which can be implemented much faster, and with less hesitation.

PHASE 3. THE EXPERIMENTAL PHASE

The Experimental Phase is when you determine *which* activity works best, and when you try different approaches. Maybe you have followed the plan outlined in the Implementation Phase but you've only lost one pound, at the end of the month. Now you know that to lose two pounds in a month, you will most likely need to spend an hour on the treadmill, 20 minutes on the elliptical and do 40 pushups. Of course, you may also need to adjust a completely different aspect of your plan, such as diet, rest and hydration, but unless you experiment, you won't know what works best for you.

Sometimes to get things going, we need to trick our brains into thinking the change we are implementing is temporary. Our mind is not known to follow orders, it only gathers information we feed it. If you make one small temporary commitment at a time, your brain won't take it as a life-changing event. The challenge is never the change itself. It's the fact that change can have a permanent impact, which is hard for our routine loving minds to accept. Our brains are more accepting of the temporary, non-threatening commitments. If you need to, tell yourself this is not a permanent change, otherwise the brain will find a way to make you so uncomfortable, and that will make you stop.

PHASE 4. HABIT ESTABLISHMENT PHASE

A habit takes almost 30 attempts to stick. A sports psychologist and the author of one of my favorite books called, *The Mind of a Champion*[1] - Julie Bell, Ph.D did an awesome study on the habits of athletes, which she talks about in her book.

She specializes in helping professional athletes get to the next level of performance, with a focus on mental toughness and discipline.

Julie Bell discusses in depth how habits are formed, and why it takes an average of 28 tries to establish a new habit. Think of a change that you wanted to make into a habit. How many tries did it take? How often do you remind your children, friends, employees or coworkers the same thing over and over again?

If it takes a professional athlete almost 30 tries to make a change permanent, how can we get frustrated and give up after only a few attempts ourselves? We need to be more patient, believe in practice, and try a minimum of 30 attempts. Make a commitment to your change, set a goal and write it down.

"I will do X daily for the next 30 days. If I do not attain the desired results, I can go back to my old ways."

I promise, if you commit to a new habit for 30 days, the results will not disappoint you, and you just might make the change permanent.

You cannot ignore certain rules during Phase 4: Habit Establishment. If you are implementing a change every other day, you must commit for 60 days. If you are implementing a change every three days, then you must commit for 90 days, and so on.

Unfortunately, we can also unconsciously develop bad habits. Most of our bad habits are developed unconsciously, because we don't develop good habits specifically, due to not having good habits in the first place. We don't just wake up one day and say, today I will start being "X". People generally don't decide to be lazy, or have a poor diet. These are the long-term results of not doing the exact opposite, which creates the unconscious bad habits, casually. One of the worst habits, is developing the habit of, "*It worked so well, I stopped doing it*" which is a term we often use in the small business world. Not too long ago my team and I were talking about this expression and one of the girls in the office said "this is true, even when it comes to drinking more water, I do a good job of drinking lots of water until I don't. I guess this saying applies to work and personal life".

We date and have great times with our partners, but after marriage and a few kids, we stop dating our spouse. There is nothing wrong with getting a babysitter and taking your spouse out on a date night at least once a month, working out together, flirting with your spouse, and buying him or her flowers. I can't tell you how many of my peers went through a divorce because what worked so well in their dating phase of the relationship, worked so well, they stopped doing them in their marriage.

I have a very successful relationship. I don't mean to brag about it, but the reason is, I always go back and ask myself, "Why did my wife fall in love with me in the first place?" Yes we change, yes, life changes and so do our circumstances, but we shouldn't change certain activities that brought us fun, pleasure, and gratification in the first place.

While change is important, leaving some things the way they are, is not necessarily a bad thing. Not everything has to change, especially the parts of your life that leaves you feeling fulfilled and content. The idea is to make changes in areas that you either want to change, improve, or get more of. It's also important to keep in mind that failure will inevitably be a part of the journey, so accept it as a required factor towards your destination.

A friend of mine once said, "Success is all past failures that you refined and put to good use."

I always refer to failures as lessons, unexpected results, opportunities, refining etc., as most of my proud accomplishments in life came from experiencing failure. I strongly believe, that you never truly learn who you are, until you have gone through great pressure, and faced situations that require you to hone your decision making and problem-solving abilities. It's critical to keep in mind that failure is always greater in our thoughts than it is in reality. When facing a potential risk, ask yourself, "How did past failures you've experienced in reality, compare to what you thought they would be like?" They were probably *never* as bad as you thought and in fact, you probably learned a lot from them.

As long as you know failing is just part of the journey, you will no longer seek to avoid failure. You can just let it be, and even see failure as practice towards opportunities that entail positive possibilities. Some say, "Luck is preparation meeting opportunity." I say that luck is practice, which includes preparation *and* failure, which later meets opportunity.

Now that you are more accepting of change, understand the comfort of being uncomfortable, and what it takes to achieve success through the F^4 formula, we can move on to the next few chapters. Next, we'll look at what it takes to cultivate the self-discipline and self-commitment to get your four tanks full to the brim.

To access more tools and resources from Hayk, visit: www.haykt. org/mindset-resources

CHAPTER TWO
SELF-DISCIPLINE

Goals of This Chapter:

- Understand the basic functionalities and limits of your mind's capabilities
- Discover how clarity leads to action
- Learn how action leads to activity
- Find out how activity brings results through routine, time and process
- Understand that there are no exceptions to certain rules of nature
- Learn some basic help tools and how easily they can be implemented

In chapter two, I will share a series of short and long definitions of some very basic tools that can be easily implemented in day to day activities. My goal with this chapter is to add some very basic but useful *tools* to your tool belt.

THE DEFINITION OF DISCIPLINE

What does discipline have to do with mind control? While there are many definitions of discipline, I like this one from Dictionary.com:

> **Discipline** *activity, exercise, or a regimen that develops or improves a skill; training.*

Activity, exercise, regimen, refine, improvement, skill, training, development, hard work, ethics, open mindedness - do these sound familiar? Maybe it's something that you need to do to achieve results in sports, the gym, your relationship, or career. Let's imagine that you are a first-time basketball player. What is the first purchase you make? Would it be shoes, or socks? Of course, you have to have a ball. If you want to, you can play barefoot, but you cannot begin without a ball. So what's the first thing you'll do with the ball? You dribble.

How do you check for ball quality? Is it in the way the ball bounced? Can you spin the ball in the air looking for consistency in weight distribution? Think of learning to dribble the ball, as developing a new habit.

You'll remember from the prior chapter that sports psychologist Julie Bell found that it took an average of twenty-eight reminders or practices to develop a habit, so it becomes second nature.

Let's say you want to learn to dribble a basketball. You may need to practice two hours per day. It will most likely take you about a month of practice to stop looking at the ball and be able to dribble, without giving the ball your full attention. That's how long it will take you to get good enough to dribble, using just muscle memory. If you don't need to look at the ball while you dribble, you will be able to look at the hoop for an open shot or look for another player to pass to, or to try your cross over or commit to another move to overtake your opponent.

With hours of practicing dribbling, passing, or shooting, you become what we call, "good" at the activity. Then, you develop your discipline, to refine your game. Then you refine your game for 10,000 hours. Your new skill becomes the familiar practice of disciplinary hard work and you become, a professional player. Of course, it's easier said than done, but no professional athlete skipped any of those steps.

When we don't achieve the results we want, it's usually because we haven't taken the required steps. We often blame others, the situation, or call it plain old bad luck.

To access more tools and resources from Hayk, visit: www.haykt. org/mindset-resources

IMPROVE YOUR FOCUS
IMPROVE YOUR
RELATIONSHIPS

A speaker at a corporate seminar I attended had us try an exercise from her recent book. We were to stare at the very tip of a pen or pencil and focus on counting to 60. If we caught ourselves having any other thought even for a *millisecond*, we'd have to start again from the beginning. After a few minutes of silence, she asked if anyone could complete the exercise, by a show of hands.

I noticed about 5% of the room raised their hands. (I personally thought they were all liars, but I'll give them the benefit of the doubt.) I consider myself to be highly disciplined and I couldn't even get close. It was a very basic but interesting experience, since it seemed like everyone was fairly easily distracted. But being distracted doesn't necessarily mean you can't focus, and it doesn't mean you aren't mentally tough. Like anything else, it's something that requires practice, as distractions are too easily overlooked in our modern day society, especially with the technology boom, full of instant notifications.

The way technology can disrupt a train of thought is absolutely bizarre. It even interrupts conversations. How often have you had your phone ring, and you completely lost your train of thought? How often have you been having a conversation, and someone stops and answers their phone? As I said, focus just like anything else takes practice, it's not a given.

You can start to focus by putting your phone on *do not disturb* at work, if it's affecting productivity. Let your close people know what you are doing, and share your work number and email in case of emergencies.

Mondays are my family days, when I do nothing but spend time with my family. Only after I started turning my smartphone off is when Mondays truly became family days. The texts or social media messages can wait.

I also recommend that you remove social media applications from your phone, and only use social media from a home computer. If you're unwilling to remove the applications at least turn OFF the notifications. That really helps narrow down the time spent looking at useless videos or reading through pointless conversations.

Focus doesn't just relate to work. Often we are so distracted that we don't necessarily bring the work home, but we bring the distraction habit home. We also bring home what we didn't finish doing because we were distracted. This can affect your relationship with loved ones, especially your spouse.

Like it or not, your job continues when you get home, because your coworkers and bosses need your undivided attention all of the time. Your most important coworker/boss, your spouse, will also need your undivided attention. A good family rule can be to put your phone in a bucket when you get home for the first couple of hours. If a client is so demanding that you must respond to them on your off time, you are better off letting that client go.

It's really difficult to have good relationships when there is nothing else you are passionate and good at. That's why you see successful married couples that have their other ducks in a row, all in one.

What de! nes you is not how you do one thing, but how you do everything.

THERE'S NO SUCH THING AS MULTITASKING

Multitasking is a myth.

However, you can get a lot done. There is a way to get a lot done without having to constantly be distracted with multiple things at once. Some people call the ability to focus on one task with such intensity that you pay attention to nothing else hyper-focusing.

The good news is that we can all learn how to hyper-focus. Let's go back to the basketball example.

In the last section, you trained your muscles through memory, to be able to dribble the ball while you run down the court. We can type on a keyboard while carrying on a conversation at the same time, or drive to work via the same route every day, and never think about directions.

However, this does not mean you are "actively" performing multiple tasks. You have two sides to your activity: the part you are paying attention to - the "active" part -- and the inactive element, which happens automatically. Some might call it operating on autopilot or second nature. You are performing something you have mastered through repetition, without giving it much conscious thought.

Several scientific studies on multitasking have come to the conclusion, that it's essentially impossible. In 2016, CNN published multiple Emmy award winner Chief Medical Correspondent Dr. Sanjay Gupta's article called *Your Brain on Multi" tasking*[1], which showed a severe decrease in ability to pay attention, as well as continue doing the activity you started with, while attempting another activity at the same time. If you view the article in the references at the end of this book you will also see a video of Dr. Sanjay explaining this.

This is why it's impossible to look for directions while driving, have a conversation with different people at the same time, or read a book and talk on the phone. All of these are active tasks, and you can't autopilot, active tasks. You simply *cannot* focus your active mind on more than one task at a time. That's the reason there are laws against using a cell phone while driving.

One of my employees claimed that she could be on a conference call while writing an email, and update her social media at the same time. So I asked her, "Are you engaged in all three tasks equally, or do you catch yourself refocusing and going back and forth?" She quickly got my point.

We have illusions thinking we can do multiple things at once, but often we are lying to ourselves. Multitasking lowers the quality in the overall output of what you are working on and often can cause more work, as the potential for errors is too high, when distracted.

To access more tools and resources from Hayk, visit: www.haykt. org/mindset-resources

HOW TO CONTROL YOUR THOUGHTS

There *are* ways to practice, controlling your thoughts. Some people use meditation, others use physical exercise or sports. Some even use vacations or staycations. It's easier said than done, but people do it every day. It's how people learn new habits, or even quit addictions like smoking or drinking.

There is one common denominator in all people that achieve positive results in the face of any mental or physical obstacle - the act of repeatedly taking intentional and disciplined action. Some naturally develop this habit, some get it through practice, and still others never tend to master discipline of their own mind. When we fail to sufficiently control our thoughts, we end up unconsciously taking actions that are detrimental to our well-being, as most of our bad habits are formed unintentionally.

Good decisions are the results of our best thoughts. Bad decisions are the results of our not so good thoughts. This is why you really have to be careful with how you occupy your mind.

Why are thoughts so important? Because thoughts turn into

decisions, which turn into actions, which turn into results which can be good or bad. So whatever it takes to reset your mind and clean out the bad thoughts, whether it's a vacation, hobby, daily breaks, naps, or exercise do not ignore what makes you happy. Occupy your mind so much with good that the bad has no room to grow.

WHY DEADLINES ARE GOOD FOR YOU

Have you ever found yourself with too many tasks needing to be completed, but still did nothing as the deadline approached? Then you rush and get 80% done in the last 20% of the time you were given? This is called the Parkinson's law which states work expands so as to fill the time available for its completion.

Have you heard of anyone claim that they perform better "under pressure?" I have found that the more pressure we are under, the more we hyperfocus on a single active task at a time. Our mind determines the most efficient and natural way to function, to help us de-stress. De-stressing means crossing off tasks from our to-do list, and it will help us manage one task at a time more efficiently.

That's why you hear people say they perform their best under the most amount of pressure, without realizing that they uncontrollably hyperfocus, under pressure. The closer we get to deadlines, the more pressure we have to focus. It's a natural survival instinct we have. Our mind does not follow orders, but it does gather information. When under a lot of pressure, your mind knows when it needs to focus.

The information at this point is the pressure you are putting yourself through, due to the deadline. The pressure increases the closer you are to the deadline. The focus that comes, is the end result of the information your mind collected. When there is no pressure, our thoughts are scattered. But when the pressure increases the closer we get to the deadline, so does our focus. This is why it is so important to always have goals and deadlines. They keep you motivated, focused and productive.

THE MARTIAN - SOLVING ONE SMALL PROBLEM AFTER ANOTHER

A very interesting viewpoint on small *problem solving* came to me when I recently watched a movie called, "The Martian." The actor Matt Damon plays Mark Watney, an astronaut stuck on Mars with very limited supplies and no help. His survival, solely depends on his creative problem-solving skills. (Warning: Skip the rest of the paragraph if you don't want to spoil the ending of the movie for yourself.) Towards the end of the movie, when Matt Damon is back on earth giving a lecture to a classroom full of students, he tells them, "You do the math, you solve one problem, then you solve the next one and then the next, and if you solve enough problems, you get to go home."

The entire movie illustrates what human beings are capable of under pressure. Clearly, Mark Watney was under an incredible amount of pressure, and when he saw a problem, his deadline was now or never, every time. He would do the math and solve the problem, which eventually brought him home.

No one is truly comfortable under pressure, so our minds help find ways for us to efficiently get to our comfort and peace, a.k.a. our home. You can use deadlines to your advantage and believe in the process, which is to solve one problem at a time and eventually you will make it *home*. The point I want to make with this movie example is we underestimate how much we can accomplish over time. The only focus we need to have is on the small victories and baby steps. Eventually we will look back and surprise ourselves because of how far we've come.

Thinking big is a huge part of staying creative and motivated, but you have to be very careful. Often when we think of the big picture, we forget that the devil is in the details. Thinking small has to be an obsession, while not forgetting the big picture of what we are working towards, as the small steps are the prerequisite, to the big goal.

One Bite at a Time
Small daily progress + Time = Big long-term results

How do you strengthen your willpower, discipline and focus?

Be goal focused, even if you struggle. We all feel that way sometimes. Being distracted is ok, it's human nature. Just make sure not to multitask. Handle a single task at a time with a common goal. Think about one daily change you can make towards a big goal. That activity has to be something you can measure in a reasonable period of time, and with noticeable results. According to Bill Gates, *"Most people overestimate what they can do in one year and underestimate what they can do in ten years."* If we look at yesterday, everything is the same as today. If we look at ten years ago, everything is different. Most of us under-estimate the power of small daily progress.

I have a small habit that made a world of difference in my productivity. I used to underestimate the power of having a daily to-do list. Now, every morning, I write down a list of what I need to do today, and work on the list one by one. If there is anything I don't get done, I carry it over to the next day and make my to-do list for the next day. It gives me a sense of direction on where to start the next day. It doesn't help to lose sleep over the "what I didn't finish for the day" items you didn't get to.

Let the piece of paper you keep your to-dos on, or your smartphone list, do the worrying for you. You can pick up where you left off the next morning, as sleep needs to be as comfortable as it can be.

To access more tools and resources from Hayk, visit: www.haykt. org/mindset-resources

THE LAW OF NO CONTROL
OF OUTCOME

WHAT IS, VERSUS WHAT WASN'T

By now, I have figured that the outcome of pretty much anything big is predetermined, and it makes no sense for me to try to control the uncontrollable. To me, these are things like the weather, terminal illnesses, death, economy, politics, how people are, or belief systems. While we can't *control* anything or anyone, we *can* influence things. The most important daily influence we can make, is the influence of our happiness. We can also influence others to be happy. The art of influencing others is nothing more than attracting likeminded people to follow your lead and implementing influence over different minded people to see things from your perspective. We can lead others towards a given situation or thought, or we can use it to our advantage, but we cannot control outcomes of the major things I mentioned above.

Let's use a simple visual example.

Try this, jump.

What happens once you reach the peak of your vertical jump? You come down. Can you control your body and prevent yourself from returning to the ground?

No. Regardless of what you think or hope or try to do, gravity will always pull you back. You can influence the height of the jump which will give you more hang time, but the outcome will always be the same.

Why such a simple example? Because true genius is in its simplicity. It's in our human nature to complicate the simplest things, and negatively influence how we feel towards our results.

Often when facing an outcome that I'm not happy with, I always ask myself the question from this example, "Am I fighting gravity?" If that's the case, I have to quickly recognize, learn my lesson, and move on. It's very demoralizing to live in regret, which can take away a lot of good opportunities that are right in front of us.

To complement the first example, here is another more relevant example. I have gone through a lot of employees in my business. Naturally, I have had to let go of a lot of employees. It's my least favorite part of my job, but when I've decided I'm going to fire someone, nothing will change my mind. Regardless of what that person is doing that day, how they are, and even if I change my mind at the last minute, because I've learned, certain interactions can interfere with my logic. I can't allow temporary emotions, talk me out of a logical decision.

At this point the decision is out of the employee's control, no matter what they say or do. I tend to establish a close enough relationship with my employees that it's not awkward keeping in touch with them long after their employment is done with me. So I have observed 3 different personality types of people that get fired, and what getting fired meant to them.

1. It's the best thing that had ever happened to this person. This person is usually very driven and motivated, but there are a million reasons why even the most driven employees get fired. They get fired mostly because of their tendency to cut corners for a bigger paycheck, or their inability to get along with others. They take the opportunity to improve, grow, and go on to become very successful somewhere else. They are so motivated that this experience ignites a fire in them, and they do whatever possible, not to ever experience getting fired again. Usually negative experiences are very emotionally impactful to this person, and they do whatever they can to avoid feeling this way. This often leads to good personal growth. This person understands they don't have control over what happened. They make the best of what happened versus living in the past, of what could have been done differently.

2. It makes no difference for this person. They don't grow, they have no regrets, and they kind of, sort of, continue living their life, like nothing happened. In most cases that's the reason why they got fired, because they didn't have much passion for the job, or for most other things. Knowing why they were fired or what they could have done differently, does not make them uncomfortable, they are too busy seeking comfort, to consider the uncomfortable opportunity of growth.

3. It's the worst thing that's ever happened to this person. They nag and complain about what happened so much so, that they grow bitter. They are too busy pointing fingers at others that they never take the chance to look in the mirror and take responsibility for

their own flaws. Negativity was probably the main reason this person was fired. They live in the regret of the past, and that job was most likely the best thing that had ever happened to them. They live a life of complaining about how unlucky they are. They are so obsessed with control, that when things don't go their way, they fixate over the negative side of things and how the world works against them, as nothing goes their way.

It's common sense not only understand, but to practice accepting that most major things are out of our control. However, we are very much in control of our happiness around those things.

Sometimes when we try something new -- a relationship, a career, a project - we develop expectations for it. Often, the reality does not meet those expectations, and when things don't go as we imagined they would, we tend to lose enthusiasm for whatever that new endeavor was. It can be helpful to realize in anything new we commit to, we're likely to face an expected result, and the only thing we can control is how we feel about it. If you can learn to be ok with the uncontrollable outcomes you can't control, you will be less emotional when things don't go your way. One of my favorite success quotes fits here perfectly,

"Success consists of going from failure to failure without loss of enthusiasm." - Winston Churchill

To access more tools and resources from Hayk, visit: www.haykt. org/mindset-resources

CHAPTER THREE

PHYSICAL SELF-DISCIPLINE, THE LAW OF COMMONALITY & THE LAW OF COMPOUNDING ATTRACTION

Goals of This Chapter:

- Learn how to strengthen your discipline
- See how the acronym CAAR provides the perfect formula for results
- Develop a method for sticking with important goals
- Learn why it's critical to delay gratification
- Learn the importance of simple common methods that always work
- Understand why and how attraction laws compound over time
- Reminder on why our physical well-being is a priority

Why is hard work so essential -- and why do the most rewarding things come so hard?

Well it's simple, if it were easy we would all have everything we wanted. A good functioning, healthy body doesn't come easily. After all, most food that's good for your body doesn't taste as good, compared to the unhealthy food injected with high doses of sugar and fat.

Most of us are or claim to be "too busy" to prepare healthy food, get enough sleep, and exercise regularly. Even when we try to catch up on these things, we usually find ourselves knocked over by the wave of life that just keeps hitting us.

How, do *some* people accomplish their fitness, friendship, family and financial goals all at the same time? It *is* feasible and replicable - but it requires discipline.

WHAT DOES IT MEAN TO BE DISCIPLINED?

Being busy and being productive are sometimes mistaken for being the same thing, but they're very different. I once heard someone say, "discipline is the act of doing what you don't want to do, when it needs to be done so you can get, what you don't have." Of course, it's easier to *plan* a disciplined activity than to execute on it. This kind of discipline requires changing habits, setting goals and schedule management.

The first habit we need to change, is our tendency to make excuses. My high school's Strength and Conditioning coach said this, when I was making excuses to cut my workout short. He said, "Excuses are like butt holes, we all got them and they all stink." More than a decade later, I still remember that sentence, and it follows me everywhere.

To access more tools and resources from Hayk, visit: www.haykt. org/mindset-resources

CAAR - THE RESULTS FORMULA

When I studied human behavior in my business practice, I had to find a way to keep my team focused towards a common goal. I came up with the 4-step results formula outlined below. I noticed over time, this formula didn't just work effectively in business, it worked with pretty much any problem solving and goal setting.

It is:

CLARITY + ACTION + ACTIVITY = RESULTS FORMULA

Think of the CAAR as the VEHICLE (pun intended) used to get you from planning to results.

This was my way to ensure the million things in my head, didn't get in the way of what I was looking to accomplish. With enough practice, I found that I could apply this formula to just about anything.

APPLYING THE CAAR FORMULA TO PHYSICAL SELF-DISCIPLINE

1. CLARITY

Let's say I want to look better. The first step is to specifically define what "look better" means to me. So, I put a number to that: I want to lose ten lbs. Then I decide how I'll do it. Perhaps I start jogging two miles per day, five days in a row and track my results. If I find that I lost one pound, then I know that I'll probably lose one pound for every ten miles I run while keeping the same diet. Knowing this number allows me to come up with a clear picture of exactly what I need to do, and what the required change measure is, to achieve the goal. This leads to the next crucial step of the formula.

2. ACTION

This is the most important step to any plan or goal. I start and repeat the process over and over. Since I lost one pound with ten miles, I now jog two miles per day for ten days, and so I'm on track to lose an average of three pounds every month. That means that I'll achieve my goal of a ten pounds weight loss, within about three months, if I do nothing else (i.e., no additional exercise or diet change.)

Now imagine how much more quickly I'd see results if I were to also incorporate a good diet program. It's common to not achieve any realistic goals when you give yourself too many at once. It's always easier to start off small, with two or three daily goals. A good rule of thumb when starting an exercise program effectively, is to add more water intake, around two liters per day, and cut as much added sugar as possible.

It's ideal to eliminate added sugar. I did that and it was simple and not too complex to start seeing noticeable results. I also learned the reason why I never started complex diet programs was the fact that they were too complicated. Start simple and get fancy later.

TAKING ACTION TO LOSE WEIGHT

When my wife and I had our first child, I gained 35 pounds during the first year of his life. I went from eight hours of sleep on average per night to four, if I was lucky. No more evening workouts, no more coming home to relax. The change was drastic, sudden, and uncomfortable, and my body fought back. My body thought I was always getting ready to run a marathon, given my daily stress level. So my body stored all the fat, sugar and toxins while lowering my metabolism.

I confused this feeling with pressure, however and like other highly motivated individuals, I assumed this pressure would bring out the best in me, so I embraced it. Most new parents, new business ventures, or other intense pressure related scenarios, have similar effects on the body and mind. But I was beginning to feel ashamed of the way I was starting to look, and worst of all, feel. I noticed that I was becoming less happy, as I continued to gain weight. My energy levels were decreasing, and I was becoming short tempered with my employees, which was completely against my belief system as an employer. I recognized the problem was my weight gain, so I made a clear decision to get my physical health *and* positivity back. The way I got back in shape all started with my ability to get clear on the fact that I needed change.

I woke up and ran two miles each morning before I went to work. Next, I integrated a better diet, fighting off my biggest craving, sweets. I stayed away from sugar six days per week and stopped myself from eating every night after 9PM, since that's when I always seemed to get the strongest cravings. I made sure to get plenty of rest on the seventh day, which I also made my "cheat meal day." I allowed myself to have any dessert I wanted.

As I began to feel better I started training longer. The thirty-five pounds were gone in five months in a very healthy way, and it never came back. This not only improved my health, but positively influenced my discipline to make similar tweaks in my business and my relationships. The life-changing habits coming out of this process were much more valuable than the thirty-five pounds I lost. The positive mental tweaks and adaptability to change, are now with me everywhere.

ACTIVITY

Repeating the action steps becomes your activity plan. Of course, a physical fitness program doesn't have to be built around running. You can use the elliptical, stairs, walking, jumping jacks, etc. The most important part, is to make it something you know you will do repeatedly and track the results - a *lifestyle change*.

- **Results**

   Once you're ten, twenty, or thirty pounds lighter - or have become more efficient at work, or have more time left at the end of each project, give yourself a moment to acknowledge that *you're there*. Don't forget, this was a short goal, but you met it. You can now set longer goals as you go, but you must still have *clarity before action, action before activity and activity before results*. Stick to the formula: CAAR (Clarity, Action, Activity and Results) in every way.

   CAAR requires determination, willpower, discipline and -

yup -- plain old fashion boring routine. So how do you get started? Commit to a minimum of 30 activities.

• Schedule It: Commit to 30 Workouts

Let's say you commit to going to the gym every Monday, Wednesday and Friday after work. You have a healthy meal when you arrive home, then go to sleep at a reasonable hour. After a few days, you don't notice results, so you either stop exercising or stop the healthy diet. It should be obvious that you've given up too soon. I highly encourage you to re-read the four Phases of Change from the end of Chapter one before moving forward. There I reference the author of one of my favorite books called, *The Mind of a Champion* - Julie Bell, Ph.D where she breaks down, forming a habit, takes 28 attempts. After going to her seminar I couldn't remember what number she said so I said 30 to myself, and when I read her book I realized I was wrong,-close enough- so I kept 30 as my rule of thumb.

So, it takes almost 30, 28, to be exact, attempts to create a healthy habit. This is no different. If your plan is to work out three days per week, then the earliest you can give up is after ten weeks (30/3=10).

That's over two months. I *guarantee* if you stick to a fair diet plan and a consistent workout schedule, you will see positive, noticeable results within 30 days, and it will be motivating enough to form a habit that will lead to *great* results later. After this, you can plan the workouts around your weekly schedule. But unless you start with the simplest plan and attempt it at least 30 times, don't bother starting.

• Why do people fail to start a new program?

Of course, it can be easy for us to find excuses to why something isn't working and give up on it before we should. Perhaps you're following a rule that states that you have to run one mile per day, but it didn't work for a friend. Or maybe *you* saw different results in the past, so you don't think this approach will bring success for you.

When I was eighteen years old, I would run one mile per day and eat all I wanted, and no matter what, my body looked great. Well now it's a whole different story two decades later, as it is for most people! I must do five times the cardio and be ten times more careful with my diet to get the same results, which were almost effortless when I was in my teens. Many other things had to change through trial and error, but that was the only way I was able to find what my now older body needed, to replicate my younger body's results. Often it's as simple - and as difficult -- as implementing a different plan. We tend to ignore the diminished value factor of what worked in the past, without taking into consideration all the changes since our last attempt, at whatever we are looking to replicate. Always track the new numbers, compare to the past and look for the difference -- then adjust accordingly. The same goes for all commitments, not just health.

To access more tools and resources from Hayk, visit: www.haykt. org/mindset-resources

THE LAW OF
COMMONALITY FACTOR

Starting and sticking to goals, is a huge part of succeeding in commitments, but you have to make sure you are headed in the right direction. If one follows a certain method or direction, the outcome will be close to the most certain predictive future results. For instance, if you like the physical build of wrestlers and want to look like a wrestler one day, you will most likely be able to replicate or come relatively close to what they look like if you start wrestling and if you exercise the way wrestlers do, with regularity. You can't start looking like a wrestler if you only power lift or swim. You can't expect to have the results of what you did not do.

There are exceptions to the law, but just like the Law of Large Numbers which essentially states that just because you do something more or less, the large number probability percentage does not change. The commonality factor is almost flawless in predicting results.

For example, we have around a 35% obesity rate in the United States, the Law of Large Numbers shows us the predictability that if we look at one million people most likely 350,000 of them are obese. The Law of Commonality Factor works the same way, you just have to understand that you cannot expect the results you are seeking unless you do the similar required work that generated those results in the first place.

This law is a branch of common sense, such as adding two + two you should expect to get four. You don't expect any other result, if you keep on adding two + two. This is the idea of not reinventing the wheel and following something that has worked in the past, it's working now, and will work in the future.

If the wheel has been invented, spend your efforts on properly installing the wheel, not reinventing it. Can you imagine if you literally had to make your own wheels from scratch for your car? How much work would that be for you? Often failure is not the lack of execution, it's in burning yourself out, and solving what has already been solved, such as making your own homemade tires. Someone has already gone through the trial and error and has come up with a good product, so that you can avoid a lot of headaches. You must get very good at not reinventing the wheel and learn to replicate working methods.

AVOID INSTANT GRATIFICATION

A hard worker with a long-term perspective that delays instant gratification, and is consistently disciplined, achieves a good career, health, and relationships. Some individuals who have arrived at this state, claim that it's second nature. They have developed habits, failure does not like (discipline, grit, positivity, etc.), therefore they have results failure does not give (abundance, happiness, good health, relationships etc.)

When are we most susceptible to instant gratification? Usually, it's when we are extremely happy and feel we deserve a reward, *or* when we're feeling down and hoping that treating ourselves, will somehow lift our moods. Yet, neither of these situations is an ideal time to make important decisions.

AVOID MAKING COMMITMENTS WHEN YOU ARE HAPPY

David gets a raise, which is a result of long-term hard work. His immediate response to the good news is happiness and excitement, both temporary feelings that his mind is not built to sustain long-term. Therefore, David defaults to seeking instant gratification, and spending the earned income, becomes easy. It satisfies his instant entitlement and satisfies his temporary wants, but can become a very nasty habit that might set him back much further than he was, before getting the raise.

So David goes and buys a car, a commitment that leads to a long-term financing contract. When that need for instant gratification, the "honeymoon" phase - goes away, David will still be left with his commitment, minus the enthusiasm of the decision. There follows regret, a struggling bank account, and no happy thoughts about the raise.

Unfortunately, it takes time to gather wisdom, usually as a result of learning from our past mistakes, and hopefully by observing others. Wisdom has no emotion, no anger, or feelings involved. So while discipline can be painful, the pain from regret is much more difficult to bear. It's not easy to delay gratification, but it's much harder to live with the long-term results, of lacking discipline (i.e., an ill-advised automobile purchase).

AVOID MAKING DECISIONS WHEN YOU ARE HANGRY (ANGRY + HUNGRY = HANGRY)

Have you ever been so hungry that you were angry? This is where the term "hangry" got its origin, and it's used often enough that we know it happens to a lot of people! Avoid making decisions in this state, as it causes short-sightedness. When you are hungry, your mind is focused on the immediate desire for food, so you tend to make irrational decisions based on negative emotions and a short temper. As hard as it can be to find the time, try having a nice meal in peace, and enjoy it so you can calm down from your busy day.

A good time to make smart decisions is when you're well fed and calm. You can probably think of a million smarter ways to spend money when you're in a more thoughtful state, perhaps investing in mutual funds or purchasing real estate.

Comprehending how instant gratification and a long-term perspective work is crucial to making and sticking to good decisions. In a way, it's good that nothing good comes easy, if it did, then we would not have the thrill of the journey, the most satisfying part of difficulty.

To access more tools and resources from Hayk, visit: www.haykt. org/mindset-resources

HOW TO SET S.M.A.R.T. GOALS TO ACHIEVE YOUR DESIRED RESULTS

"Winging it" - whatever "it" is -- without a plan simply doesn't work. Setting a goal helps you get very deliberate about your activity, which in return helps you become more productive. So whatever your game plan, always start by *writing it down.* Don't type, actually use a pen and write it on a piece of paper. There is a certain strength to your creativity that is enhanced when you write on a clean piece of paper that you won't get with typing.

Also, avoid using paper with lines, our mind likes a clean surface, as it gives more ownership. Get a clear sheet of printing paper to write your S.M.A.R.T goals down.

We use the acronym S.M.A.R.T to signify that your goals are:

- **Specific.** You can describe the details. (For example, *I want to complete a full marathon.*) - This is how I committed to my first marathon.
- **Measurable.** You can measure the goal using either quantitative or qualitative assessments. (*To complete a*

marathon, I need to run 26.2 miles in less than six hours).

- **Achievable.** You can achieve the goal. (*Why not, millions have done it and it's de! nitely achievable if I train enough, and give myself enough time. I already exercise and am in good physical shape.*
- **Realistic.** The goal is realistic given existing constraints, such as time and resources. (*The marathon is in ! ve months, currently I can run six miles without stopping. It's very achievable to add one extra mile per/ week for the next 20 weeks.*)
- **Time-limited.** You must achieve the goal within a specified time frame. (*Given the 20 weeks' timeframe, it's not enough to be able to run 26.2 miles, but I need to average a 12 Minute per mile pace or quicker so I can ! nish in the given six hours. I will run at a 12- minute per mile pace, a couple of miles per day for ! ve days. On the sixth day, I will add an additional mile to my longest run and rest on the seventh day. With this plan I will start tomorrow.*

This is the exact formula my friend Brian Harris and I followed when he reached out to me and committed to join me for my next marathon. A marathon was one of his life goals. He had never ran more than five miles at once before. He was in good shape to begin with, so we drew it out and added one mile per week. We stuck to the program and Brian did his first marathon in June of 2018 in four hours 30 minutes, like a champ. I was proud of him, beyond words.

HOW TO SET ATTAINABLE GOALS YOU CAN KEEP

I have found the S.M.A.R.T approach to be the best in helping to clarify and simplify my goals. Completing a study on productivity, Franklin Covey came up with a great way to set and achieve goals, which I implemented in both my business and personal life. They call it the Four Principles of Execution[1] (you can get more details from their website: www.franklincovey.com)

- **Discipline # 1: Identify your W.I.G (Widely Important Goals)**

The idea here is to *focus* your finest effort on the one or two goals that will make all the difference, instead of giving mediocre effort to dozens of goals. Without focus, the other three Principles won't be able to help you. The more goals, the less achievement you'll attain -- especially achieving with excellence.

- **Discipline # 2: Act on Lead Measures**

Discipline Number two is where you leverage your activity. "Lead measures" are simply the way you gauge the activities most connected to achieving the goal - your activities' actionable step. This step requires you to define the daily or weekly measures, the achievement of which will lead to the goal. Then, each day or week, you identify the most important actions that will drive those lead measures.

- **Discipline # 3: Compelling Scoreboard**

This can be a simple design you draw on a blank piece of

paper or a whiteboard. The board should be fun and have a theme, like an animal theme, superhero theme, or sports theme, as long as it's something you enjoy. Scoreboards are crucial, since that's how we interpret games. You need a scoreboard so you can track if you are winning. You might feel your favorite sports team won the game even though they actually lost, but it always comes down to what the scoreboard says.

- **Discipline # 4: Create a Cadence of Accountability**

This is where you build a daily tracker that should consist of points. If your goal is to do with fitness, then you can track food intake and exercise time. You need to create categories as well. Say each glass of water you drink is five points, each ten minutes spent running equals ten points, and each meal you cut in half and eat in two sessions is another five points. Whatever it is, it should be simple and easy to manage daily. After a week of data collection, you'll be able to discern a reasonable points goal per week. Break it down to daily points, and work your way to that weekly goal.

Additionally, for every day you hit your daily goal, reward yourself with a token. Collect the tokens throughout the week and at the end of the week count how many tokens you have. Create a basket with drawings in it. For your fitness goal, it might be a cheat meal which can include multiple "rewards" like ice cream, chocolate, gift card to a restaurant, wine etc. You choose what you put in the basket.

You can even put a few drawings of pushups and sit-ups to mix things up. If you hit your goal seven times that week, then you get seven drawings. However, you ideally shouldn't hit your goal more than three - five times. If you're constantly and easily getting to 100%, then odds are you aren't challenging yourself enough!

Do the drawing weekly, track and tweak. It will be a no-brainer after a while and you will wonder why you didn't start this game sooner.

To access more tools and resources from Hayk, visit: www.haykt. org/mindset-resources

THE COMPOUNDING LAW
OF ATTRACTION

Many people are familiar with the Law of Attraction[1], which states that "like attracts like," or things of matching vibration are attracted to each other. I'm going to add a word to that and call it the *Compounding* Law of Attraction. Like *does* attract like; but what happens over an extended period of time when things are repeated? It compounds, like a snowball rolling down a hill. It gets bigger and faster and as it rolls, its increasing surface area collects more snow.

In the investment world, the best way to achieve large gains over time is to have an investment portfolio. My mentor Dan Sevier and I were recently discussing the stock market and he said something that really resonated with me, "It's not timing the market that you gain from, it's time *in* the market that always wins." Essentially, if you do something good over the long-term, you will always enjoy positive results, but if you're waiting for the "right" time and place to start, that elusive "perfect moment," then you have a very small chance to win.

The Compounding Law of Attraction brings people from no results, to some results, to fair results, to good results, to *very* good results, to great results, to extraordinary results, and so on. Compounding makes it exponentially difficult to go backward, once you are on a consistent pattern. Of course there can be exceptions, but easy come easy go, hard-earned hard taken away. It's the beauty of the bigger and better. Unfortunately, it can work in the opposite direction, from bad all the way down to extraordinarily bad, which I call a compounding failure.

For example, one day you wake up bitter but do nothing about your mood. You don't call a mentor, you don't listen to music, you don't read a good book, you don't exercise, you don't meet a friend for a coffee. You pretty much avoid all the things that get you into a good mood. With time you get bitterer. You become increasingly bitter with time, as what used to get you in a good mood sounds too frustrating to do now. Over more time, you start believing the world works against you, with more time you become comfortable with the thought of being bitter and angry. Others including yourself start believing you are a bitter and angry person, and it becomes a challenge to maintain positive thinking.

All actionable steps in anything you do, say, or think, lead to habits and that has a compounding effect. This compounding effect is what allows you to see where people are, over time. When you look at someone, you're always looking at the *result of their compound*. Have you ever had a friend that you were very similar to at one point in your life, but due to time and different choices, you have become completely different people? Everyone knows someone like this, maybe it's a friend whose life is the complete opposite of yours, or a colleague who has taken an entirely different career path. This is the compounding effect of a choice that was made at one point that changed your path of who you or your friend became, sometimes towards better, sometimes towards worse.

If you don't do your best, you can alter your entire life by allowing compounding to create a reality for you. There is only so much effort you can put toward influencing who you are before the compound takes over the direction you are headed. Laziness, for instance, is something that develops by one day deciding to do a bit less, then less, then even less yet again, to the point that you become someone who lives to do everything, "much less."

People who give their best every day, attain what they do through a compounding habit that improved with time. Their results grow increasingly more impressive, and can appear almost unachievable to someone looking and wondering, "How can I ever do what *they* did?" Well, it won't happen right away, it's the daily focus that compounds over time and brings forth extraordinary results that usually surprise the achiever.

THE COMPOUNDING LAW OF PUSHING AWAY THINGS THAT DON'T MATTER

How would you like to attract attractive, positive, willing to help and supportive people in your life? Focus on yourself first. Instead of trying to bring the right people into your life, *become* the right person, and they will find you. We only attract who and what we are, never who and what we want. Even if you have accidentally brought the wrong person in your life, comfort and time has a way of moving that person out. Don't wait for the "right time," the stars never align in quite the way you think they're going to, so the best time to make good decisions is always before you are reminded to.

To access more tools and resources from Hayk, visit: www.haykt. org/mindset-resources

CHAPTER FOUR
SELF-COMMITMENT

Goals of This Chapter:

- Appreciate that understanding the key to Self-Discipline is Self-Commitment
- Learn what it means to stick to your belief system using the 2+2=4 Formula
- How to develop a laser like focus
- Understand the danger of getting addicted to the pain of progress
- See projects to completion

SELF-COMMITMENT

How committed are you to yourself? If I support your commitment and agree to match it, how much commitment would I have? Keep this in mind, if you want others to invest in you- you have to invest in yourself first because people will only contribute by matching. If you're only 55% committed to the goal you've chosen, then how would you expect my 100% commitment? It's as if a commander of an army wants his troops to follow him into a war but he's only "sort of" looking for a victory. Unless you have bought into your own idea, you cannot expect others' full effort into following you.

People don't quit relationships, jobs, or memberships because of the organization, the industry or the conditions, they quit because of the people. It's most common for people to quit the leader, who misguides the team. I've found that you can commit to a big picture, but small-minded people can lead you to give up. These selfish, negative individuals can kill your big dreams with their mediocre ambitions and the continuous reminders why you shouldn't bother to shoot for the stars, since it's failure waiting to happen. They are correct when they assume you can fail, as it's the story of their life, but they are wrong in assuming you have the same fate as they do.

Never forget, no one will give you what you want, they will give you what you *are*, which won't be much if you're not fully invested in yourself. It all comes down to the standard set by you, what others see and feel around you. I have seen countless people fail at commitments, whether they had to do with their health, relationship or business, due to a lack of self-belief and faith. They didn't have 100% buy-in or 100% commitment.

I've helped a lot of peers with their startups and business endeavors, and have observed the same pattern across the board in doing so. The fully committed ones believed in what they did so much that they lost themselves in their business. They enjoyed their work so much that work felt like a hobby that they enjoy and when you do something with a lot of joy you get very good at it and see things to excellence and completion. Their potential showed, and when they interacted with clients, their clients couldn't help but want to do business with them, partially due to the level of passion they expressed.

These committed individuals seemed to usually just "vacuum"

good paying customers into their businesses and made it look effortless. Again, it's easy to follow someone so committed to themselves. The "kind-of-sort-of" committers however, the ones who weren't as committed -- that just wanted to have the title of entrepreneur or business owner, got consumed in working too hard, and complaining about it. The negative attitude they displayed in front of potential clients from the whirlwind, drove away paying customers, leading their businesses to failure. It came pretty clear upon observation who makes things work and who lets things fail. Something like marriage doesn't just magically work on its own. If you don't tend to it, it will fail. You can't be 90% committed to marriage and expect 100% success.

This is a great time to review **C.A.A.R.: (Clarity - Action - Activity - Results)** -- which is an extremely important tool I introduced in Chapter Three -- that helps to maximize the probability of positive outcome. We need 100 % "buy in" from the people whose support we need to make this idea a reality. There is a connection between how people hear an idea and how they process it. If you hear an idea that connects to your beliefs and commitments, that's an idea you'll likely admire and support. This is why it's important to surround yourself with the right people. It's possible to have someone who can talk a good game and share unhelpful information that you might actually believe if they demonstrate confidence, facts, and "reasoning" behind their claims. Unfortunately, these people have the potential to negatively alter your belief system. I had a friend who developed a very negative view of faith in God and became totally against religion. He wanted to find information that supported the way he felt *after* he decided he felt this way, so he started researching all kinds of facts and philosophy, on why religion is fake.

. . .

He had all kinds of facts and stories to shut people down when religion came up, and there were times when even I almost believed him, despite the fact that my faith is stronger than that. If something sounded good but doesn't sit right with your belief system, and in a way, gives you a bad "gut" feeling, that's a good time to go with your intuition and block off the facts. You often need to conduct a self-check on your own values and beliefs to see if you truly agree, no matter how compelling the "facts" sound.

TEST YOUR BELIEF SYSTEM WITH THE 2+2 = 4 FORMULA

No matter how you add two plus two, the answer will always be four.

If someone tells you that two plus two equals five, you will assume they're doing something wrong. The purpose of this formula is to remind yourself to have a belief system you stand by, no matter what others say. Don't change your already working formula. It's a simple metaphor to remind yourself that there was a point when you developed your principles and belief system. When someone tells you otherwise, stand strong behind it because often, others question, for no other reason, than to test how strong your belief system is. If hard work has always driven positive results in anything you have done, don't change this approach just because you see some who got lucky doing something the easy way. You can try what they say, but if their formula outcome does not match your results, always go back to your initial belief system.

If your whole life, you believed 2+2 = 4 and some future research proved otherwise, would you doubt the decisions you had made in the past that depended on this belief? Probably, but you were so certain at the time, that you made many good choices that led to good things, based on that belief. So truly, the only kind of "wrong" belief system is failing to believe in yourself.

So how do you apply the 2+2 formula to become 100% committed? Laser Focus.

LASER FOCUS

Most people tend to think like a light, with our thoughts spread over a surface area, a large body delivering visibility, but not penetration. We take on a lot of obligations at once, but only commit about 80% to all of them. Then when they never blossom, we think of ourselves as failures. However, when you focus the same light through a magnifying glass, you can burn small objects with it. When you concentrate the same light further, you can focus it to a microscopic laser level, which can cut through pretty much any hard material known to man.

Unless you have this kind of laser focus on your goals, you will not get results in the intentioned manner that, you want. General thoughts and ideas bring general results. You need *speci! c* ideas to penetrate a surface. For instance, I always wanted to be a business owner growing up. However, that was a very general and confusing commitment. So I focused on my second business professional endeavor, which was becoming involved in the insurance business. This lead to actionable steps. The **C.A.A.R** formula played a huge role in this commitment. I was **C**lear on passing my insurance license tests, which lead to me taking **A**ction and starting an agency, that lead me to the **A**ctivity of opening the agency and conducting the necessary work to attract clients, and finally that brought me the **R**esults of a good business.

Having a 100% belief is powerful but it can be 100% bad if it's focused in the wrong place. I have seen committed entrepreneurs with terrible business plans make it work through blood, sweat and tears, because no matter what others said, their commitment and belief of succeeding was always 100%. I have seen couples with every possible reason to fail figure it out, because they had a 100% belief and commitment to making their marriage work.

I call this the *Law of Occupancy*, which I discuss in further detail in Chapter five. This basically states that we only have X amount of space in anything we do at any given time. Depending on how much of the controllable space we occupy, like pouring water into a cup, the rest will be occupied by the uncontrollable opposite, for this example, it's air. The cup is never half full or half empty. The other half always has the competing opposite. Your mind works the same way. Depending on how you are occupying it, the competing opposite will fill up the difference you leave empty.

The easiest way to get rid of the air from a half full cup, is to add more water. Imagine how creative you have to get to try to get rid of the air, it's physically impossible. Now think of how we try to fix being pessimistic, negativity, failure or adversity. Often it's easier not to focus on the opposite, but to pour more good, so the bad has no room to occupy.

When working with others, the self-discipline rule is only fully effective when you're committed 100% and the other party is 100% bought in. I'm using two people for this example, but it can be a whole army. This is how two people can get four people's worth of results, while 100% committed. When you hear less is more, it truly is.

Commitment+Belief: (100% commitment + 100% belief) x (2 people) = 400%

But since people usually don't give 100%, it's common to see mediocre effort, and mediocre results, which in some ways is good, because it allows the exceptional people to shine. People who give short of the maximum, or even just the minimum, reach "their" goal, which is their standard. This was a problem in my own business at one point. We were overstaffed, but we were hitting our goals every month. Too many employees made my expense ratio too high, I was overpaying for mediocre individual performance for what seemed to be a successful practice, and it was hurting me financially. When I learned to begin using the commitment and belief rule, I cut my staff in half and increased production, which resulted in more than double net income for me.

The numbers above compound with time, and either become multipliers or dividers. In good cases, our lives formulas multiply, and over time we are shocked by our own positive results. Of course, the opposite happens for those who don't have faith in, and aren't committed to what they are doing. Their results are divided over and over until there is nothing left to divide... leading to failure.

A WORKAHOLIC MENTALITY DOES NOT EQUAL SELF-COMMITMENT

My mentor Ali Alyazdi once said, "You can be the hardest working farmer in the desert, and will never achieve even the laziest farmer's results on rich soil."

The American work ethic trains us to believe that if we put our noses to the grindstone day-after-day, hour-after-hour, we are proving to ourselves and to others, that we are committed to success. But we confuse working relentlessly towards a desired outcome as a sign of our commitment, and discover after considerable time, that we rarely arrive at our desired outcome. Consequently, we give up, and it seems as if we were never truly committed to seeing the journey through.

The problem is that we were never truly committed to achieving our desired outcomes, we were just committed to hard work. We weren't working smarter, we were only working *harder*. In most cases working smarter means putting the effort towards the right thing, like the farmer checking to make sure they are planting on good quality soil, and not only focusing on the labor.

Sometimes even the best-intentioned people (myself included) end up becoming workaholics. This was a huge realization for me. I always assumed hard work would beat talent. Occasionally it does, but being in the right place is a big part of success. You can work your butt off for a long time, but with time if the opportunity doesn't start working for you, then you will hit a wall.

DON'T GET ADDICTED TO THE PAIN OF PROGRESS

Wanting the next thing so badly that we focus on a desire for *progress,* can prompt us to start a habit of not seeing things through to completion. Often, the journey towards progress can be the best part of commitments which is why we love progress so much, but there is a fine line between enjoying progress and being addicted to it. Enjoying progress is when you are so into the journey that you finish what you start. Being addicted to progress is when you never finish what you start as the excitement of new progress is always on your mind so before you see things through you jump onto the next venture.

I can recall a time in my life when I confused the relevance of results and progress, which I later learned is the same as the difference between pleasure and pain. It began when I first tasted financial success. I remembered the past as being more pleasant than it actually *was*, and would subconsciously forget certain bad feelings and experiences. I remembered the family, financial, fitness or friendship success, but I conveniently forgot the painful early mornings, the meals I skipped during fourteen-hour work days, and late evenings that simply became what I'd gotten used to. Money-generating activity would have me so focused on the progress of grinding more and more, I became in a way, addicted to the pain of progress. I got so comfortable being uncomfortable that it became an addiction.

There is a fine line between being comfortable with the uncomfortable and being *addicted* to discomfort. As I've stated throughout the book so far, we *need* to do uncomfortable things that we have never done, to get where we have never been. Being uncomfortable is huge part of learning and developing yourself. However, we must carefully approach our habit developing activities. I was so hooked on attaining things that were equivalent to financial success, I had taken my eyes off success completely. This taught me a valuable lesson, being able to afford material things, is far from being successful.

What I was missing was the allocation of energy, which was the key. (In Chapter one, I share the (F4) Formula, which gave me the answer to where and how to distribute all my time and efforts.) I had made the mistake of getting so caught up in what I *thought* was good for me, that I was addicted to making progress in only one aspect of my life. It led to the exact *opposite* of what I truly wanted, a balanced life.

This is how I realized that the habit of getting things started had become a bad habit.

Being addicted to progress prevents people from getting to the finish line. Temporary defeat and discouragement tends to make you quit early and want to move on to the next thing, because this progress is not bringing you excitement anymore. With time, your enthusiasm wanes, your energy is tapped out, and you fail to realize that your desired result is right around the corner. Keep in mind *temporary defeat is progress,* it only becomes permanent defeat when you let the temporary defeat be the end of the road.

This addiction to pain of progress is a blind spot that we all need to be aware of. It's something to keep in mind and look out for as you work towards your goals. Look at your last few commitments, did you give up too easily, or commit too quickly to something else when things started getting difficult? Be cautiously optimistic when approaching a commitment, be aware that it can feel boring or painful at times, and make you want to jump into something more fun. But often, it's those moments of "boredom or pain" that drive the majority of results.

To access more tools and resources from Hayk, visit: www.haykt. org/mindset-resources

CHAPTER FIVE
SELF-POSITIVITY AND THE LAW OF OCCUPANCY

Goals of This Chapter:

- Understand YOUR true root of happiness
- Teach your mind to only think of positive thoughts
- Remove any space for negative thoughts to occupy your life.
- Use positive thinking to overpower adversity every single time
- Practice, hold and shoot positivity
- Use CAAR (Clarity, Action, Activity, Results) to achieve a positive mindset.

DON'T BE THE MOTH THAT FLIES TO THE FLAME

I talk a lot about how 98% of negative thoughts and fears of the future, are based on illusions which never take place. I repeat this quote to myself from time to time, "If you want to live in fear, live in the future, if you want to live in regret, live in the past, if you want to be happy, live in the present."

So why do we resort to fear of the future? Why do we slow down to see an accident on the side of the road, although we know we can't influence the outcome? It's in our human nature to be attracted to chaos and keep worst-case scenarios in our minds, although odds of that "worst case" coming to fruition is nominal. No one wants to discuss calm and peace, we want adrenaline, something that excites us and raises our blood pressure.

Being attracted to chaos and excitement is a natural human reaction, but realizing it's not helpful, can be the difference between you controlling your conditions versus, your conditions controlling you (and your life). This is why it's especially important to be aware of the type and quality of information you allow into your mind.

For example, if you want to have and show more gratitude, you need to *have a gratitude mindset ! rst,* and the condition of having more gratitude will follow. If you think buying that boat you've always wanted will make you happy, then you're probably wrong, because it will only give you temporary excitement. You will feel exactly the same after the excitement fades away, because the boat is the condition. Happy people with nice boats were happy before the boats, and will be happy without them. Conditions and possessions don't bring happiness, mindset does.

To access more tools and resources from Hayk, visit: www.haykt. org/mindset-resources

THE LAW OF OCCUPANCY

In my late teens, I developed a love for attaining material things. I wanted fancy clothes and fancy cars, and assumed these things would bring me happiness. This was my definition of success. I had no room for any extra thoughts on the matter. I had become so consumed by this that I became negative and jealous of others. That's when I realized I had to let go of these thoughts to make room for being coachable, positive, and optimistic about my opportunities in life. I came up with something I called The Law of Occupancy, which I first mentioned in Chapter four. Simply put, empty space is always filled by the opposite, so if your positive thoughts do not fill 100% of your mind, the negative will always take up the difference. If you are only 50% positive, you are only positive *half* the time, the other half, you are negative.

We often approach outside information without any "caution", and don't appreciate what "useless information" does to us. The amount of information we're constantly exposed to is not necessarily a good thing. None of us are immune to the rule of occupancy, all we control is the thought and the intake of the information. Our minds do not function well under uncertainty, since uncertainty tolerates volatility, randomness, and risk. When faced with an excess of irrelevant or insignificant information, we become poor decision makers. If we don't have good thoughts, bad will find a way in. If we don't have plans and a schedule, laziness and procrastination will find a way in. The best approach, therefore, is to occupy as much of the space as possible with only the good and the positive, so negative has no space.

YOUR THOUGHTS SPREAD LIKE WILDFIRE

It can, however, be harder to get rid of negative thoughts than to create happy thoughts. One technique is to focus on *why* the thought is negative. Sometimes, this leads to more negative thoughts as if you are pouring more gasoline into the fire. Over time, there's even a tendency to feel as though you have no control, call yourself "unlucky", and let this state of mind define you.

Positive affirmations only work when the negative is not present. This keeps the focus solely on the positive, without wishing for less of the negative. As a matter of fact, self-control is at its strongest when you can eliminate negative thoughts completely. I'm sure you've heard the saying that you should, "count your blessings." Very few people actually do this, but it really works.

POSITIVE THINKING EXERCISE:

Try counting the first ten positive thoughts you can think of. If a negative thought sneaks in, even for one second, start over. Do your best to eliminate the bad thought, and create the habit of doing so. Of course, this will take practice. This technique helps you control and maintain positivity so well, that you will be able to convert negative thoughts or experiences, and eventually be able to look at any problem *not* as a problem, but as an opportunity. Positive thinking doesn't occur with just one thought, it's the practice and consistent repetition that makes it a habit. But once you master it, you will be surprised by the problems that go away and new opportunities that present themselves.

Think about what controls your thoughts, mood, and energy. Where do your positive or negative thoughts originate? Being aware is a start, but the proper direction of power is crucial. The other day, I came across a quote while purchasing new tires:

"Power is nothing without control."
~ Pirelly, The Tire Company.

It might be a strange place to find an inspiring quote, but it resonated with me and I'm also going to add that *control* of power, is the first part. This tire manufacturer is claiming that you can have all the horsepower you want, but without the traction provided by a good set of tires, you may crash, have accidents or clock poor track times. In the same way, you should monitor proper delegation of controlled power to affect both positive and negative energy. This has a lot to do with your emotions.

SO WHAT IS EMOTION?

I think of emotion as your *energy in motion*. Operating at a higher level of performance or frequency begets positive energy (love). The exact opposite is *demoting* energy, which is to lower energy motion to its lowest form of negative thought (hate).

Understanding how this works and recognizing our "blind spots" is a crucial step towards controlling any kind of personal power or energy. Do you get negative? Do you judge others, or get short tempered? Do you feel opposite of good from time to time? Any thought that's the opposite of love or good is a negative vibrating emotion, which leads to the seven deadly sins, which I will dive into detail, in Chapter six; pride, envy, anger, laziness, covetousness, gluttony and lust. When you engage in any of these, you are essentially suffering from mental obesity.

So if we know these are bad, why do we give in? Educating ourselves is one way to prevent this. Without knowledge, we can't strategize, and without strategy, we can't execute.

Do you recognize mental sickness, obesity, disease, parasite, negative energy in motion? Do you know your strengths? Do you recognize what you need to do more of, and what to stay away from? If it's hard for you to do this for yourself, ask someone close to you, your spouse or your best friend. Chances are, they might be able to spot these things better than you can. If you have felt something, or caught yourself doing something negative, your loved ones have seen it for years. We can be both, our own worst critics and at the same time, our own best flatterers. It can be scary, but try asking someone close to you what they think your strengths and weaknesses are. Our thoughts, whether good or bad, can enable or disable us, cure or sicken us, make us or break us.

OPTIMISTIC AUTOSUGGESTION

Emile Coue was a French psychologist and pharmacist who introduced a popular method of psychotherapy and self-improvement based on optimistic autosuggestion. The Coue method is a popular conscious, mantra-like autosuggestion that mentally ill patients had to routinely repeat to heal themselves. It was,

"Every day, in every way, I'm getting better and better."

Patients said these words as many as twenty times per day, especially at the beginning, and at the end of each day. Coue's method healed many of his mentally ill patients, and his method made him famous. When asked if he was a healer, his response was, "I have never cured anyone in my life. All I do is show people how they can cure themselves."

This study shows the power that our mindset can truly have. If you understand how powerful our mind can be when we develop a habit of positive thinking, the sky's the limit. If positive self-talk can heal psychological illnesses, it can absolutely heal bad habits, negativity, fear, and other mental limitations we've developed over time. Action becomes easy, once you recognize what's holding you back. This is why it's a good idea to ask someone close to you what they believe your weaknesses and strengths to be, since this can be a blind spot for many of us.

To access more tools and resources from Hayk, visit: www.haykt. org/mindset-resources

THE POWER OF YOUR WILL

Sometimes science and facts don't make sense. Things happen that aren't supposed to. The sick person given a month to live, lives for another 20 years. The paralyzed patient that's never supposed to move starts walking again. The kid with a learning disorder in middle school, becomes a world-famous scholar. Science is crucial to life and society, but not always accurate in its predictions. Although we look for scientific proof to believe in things, faith can be more of a fact than anything else, when nothing makes sense. When the mind and the body are in harmony and both are healthy, unexplainable things happen, some of which fly in the face of what science has proven. These are usually the effects of a long-term belief system that comes with daily consistent faith.

SECRETS BEHIND SUCCESSFUL PEOPLE

New routines and habits usually begin with the recognition of the issue and starting daily positive exercises. I have asked countless successful entrepreneurs for the reasons behind their success. Surprisingly, while some knew, some didn't. Some cited hard work, others said it was their perspective. However, I've noticed a pattern in all successful people I have met in my personal and business life, and they all had the following two things in common.

A POSITIVE STATE OF MIND

The successful, healthy people I've encountered, all had very positive operative energy. No matter how bad things got, they would keep an optimistic perspective. Seeing how these kinds of people operated prompted me to come up with a saying, "nothing happens as planned, everything happens towards the better." Remember, most outcomes are not entirely controllable, they're merely influence-able. When faced with an undesirable outcome, a pessimist "beats himself up", while an optimist finds an "opportunity" or thinks of it as a lesson learned.

U.P.R. - UNCONDITIONAL POSITIVE RESULTS

Unconditional positive results are what happens to people who operate according to a simple belief system that no matter what the outcome of your actions are, you always find the positive. We've already discussed how failure is a great way to learn. When we can begin to accept disappointments as lessons, we can start looking forward to life's challenges.

Over time, we build our outlook around what we've come to expect. A positive person looks at bad experiences as a chance to get better, while a negative person wonders why bad things keep happening to them and ignores the good. Most truly successful people have a story of personal struggle and how they overcame it. They come out of it stronger and smarter. All of the successful entrepreneurs I know listen to audiobooks in their cars. They ask questions when stuck, and seek mentorship. They never stop learning and getting better. They remain a student of life at all times.

These are all techniques our minds need to stay up to date on, to maintain good mental shape. My own morning routine of reading and listening to good audiobooks has dramatically improved my attitude, and positively impacted my personal growth. I used to have an 80 minute commute to my office. Though I live much closer now, I actually miss the 160 minute daily drive time. I would listen to many positive audiobooks and podcasts in my car and I actually *looked forward* to my commute. This positively influenced my team as well. I would walk into the office fired up, wanting to share something new I'd learned several times per week. The same went for my journey home. My wife always appreciated hearing what I had learned from my daily self-education. Of course, I would have dreaded that time if I paid attention to the rush hour traffic or just listened to music.

One way to hone this habit and training to look for the positive in things, is to use the C.A.A.R. approach, (Clarity leading to Action, Action leading to Activity and Activity leading to Results) I introduced in Chapter three.

Clarity (Do you know what you want?)

This is a short and simple step. Ask yourself, are you clear that you need to work on something, for example, becoming more positive? If Yes then move on, if No then work on becoming 100% clear by soul-searching and asking others for feedback.

Action (Execution)

Commit, execute and start the actual process of counting your blessings, looking for opportunities in adversity and catching yourself when having negative thoughts. Track how many times you complain per day, and how many times you look for the positive. I made a commitment to my spouse that when I felt like complaining, I'd stop what I was doing and text her a short description of what was making me upset. Eventually, she started doing the same, and with time, we grew more positive together. Sometimes it's as simple as smiling more often, complimenting others, and making them smile. Uplifting people, is a great way to be uplifted yourself. As Mahatma Gandhi famously said, "Be the change you want to see in the world." Bring positivity to yourself by bringing it to others first.

Activity - (Activation of the process)

Activation is the day-in and day-out daily process you put together. Committing to a life-changing decision requires you to stick to a daily practice to maintain a fresh mind, and muscle memory. Harvard and Oxford-educated Professor Angela Duckworth has done very interesting research, and written a book on denominators of success called, *Grit*[1]. She studied groups of salespeople in an attempt to identify, who made the most money. She looked at the police academy to determine which characteristic would keep cadets in the industry the longest. Duckworth cited during her TED-Speech, "one characteristic that emerged as a significant predictor of success. It wasn't social intelligence, good looks, physical health, and it wasn't IQ, it was grit."

But what *is* grit? Duckworth defines grit as "the disposition to pursue very long-term goals with *passion* and *perseverance*. Grit is sticking with things over the long term and working very hard to maintain them. Grit is living life like it's a marathon not a sprint." The ability to stick to a decision and see it through to its end, is what makes the difference for countless groups of people, and areas of life. Activity is the condition of moving and getting things done towards a goal. The word itself indicates that something is alive, it's moving, it's progressing.

We can all develop a habit of starting something but never finishing it. I'm guilty of this myself. There have been instances where I've felt motivated to start something new, and then do it, but if I don't see immediate results, I hit a wall and stop. I would compare myself to my peers that never attempted to start new habits, so I mistakenly thought I was a step ahead by having execution, which they lacked. Unfortunately, not only did I fail at improving my situation, I also wasted effort and energy. As I've stated before, it's worse to have a habit of not finishing things, than the habit of not starting in the first place, since the time and effort you wasted, takes attention away from other things that demand your attention such as health, family, friends and real work.

Results - The outcome (The condition)

By this point, you have been implementing a plan long enough for the change to be physically and mentally noticeable. This is when others observe your outcome, and maybe even start to get a little jealous of you! You might even find yourself asking, "Wasn't that me a year or two ago, measuring success based on what *someone else* had done?" It's a much better feeling to be measuring yourself on your own standards, and then exceeding those standards.

To access more tools and resources from Hayk, visit: www.haykt. org/mindset-resources

SELF-DEFENSE WITH POSITIVE THINKING

Human beings are given a standard set of tools to use in everyday life. Adversity is actually one, but a much stronger weapon that can win the battle against adversity, is positivity. This tool is so powerful that any sign of bad weapons such as stress, worry, anger, laziness, lust, jealousy, will be instantly vaporized with just one pull of the trigger.

One evening I was sitting in my office alone. It was 10PM, and my team had left hours earlier. This was my first year in the business, so I was still developing my systems and processes. I felt stressed out, and felt that I didn't have enough hours in a day to keep up with everything. I can recall that this day in particular was not a good one for me. We were not meeting any of our monthly goals. To add to the load my construction business was having issues as well. We had issues on a construction project that was going to cost me a lot of time and money, and my manager at the time wanted to quit. I had no idea if I was going to afford payroll the following week, and the weekend was packed with family get-togethers that I was not in the mood for, nor had the energy to attend.

As part of the temporary agreement I had with the parent corporation of my insurance agency, I had to perform on a very high level my first year. The corporate board had to like me, and I had to maintain a full staff while I was at it. During the beginning of the office production phase, it became a company requirement to obtain a mortgage license to provide a one-stop shop service for clients on their combined insurance, investments and mortgage needs.

I had three reviews during the first year; at the three-month, six-month, and nine-month marks. I learned during my last review that the company was very happy with my numbers and competence, and would have no problems issuing my contract. The very next morning, I got a call from the executive in charge of my contract telling me that they had, as he stated, "jumped the gun." They could *not*, in fact, issue my contract as since my agreements stated that I had to carry all the required company licenses. When I had started it had become a requirement to obtain a mortgage license for which I thought I would be an exception for as it was not required before my start date. I had been so busy with production that I never even looked into this new requirement.

My birthday was rapidly approaching, which meant a mandatory professional license renewals were coming due. My existing securities and insurance licenses were due for renewal, a time consuming process I was not looking forward to. I had three months to pass my mortgage exam and keep up with current production numbers. At the time, out of everyone on my contract I was the top producer in the entire Pacific Northwest. The region was huge and included six states -- but that just meant more pressure. I needed to give 12 hours of my undivided daily attention just to continue to maintain the current lever of production.

I never felt so much pressure in my life, and the more I thought about it, the more I stressed. On top of everything, I was in the last phase of an important loan modification process that would save our home, where I lived with my parents, from foreclosure. If the loan modification didn't work, we would all be on the street. Although I was bringing in home decent money it wasn't enough to feed everyone and keep up with all the bills as my father's construction business had tanked with the housing market crisis of 2009. My parents didn't speak English to get work, and my brother was too young while still in school, so I had a lot of pressure to provide and make things work. I was learning that the insurance industry is not a get rich quick business, its get rich very slow as you don't make a lot of money when you write a lot of business, you make money after you have years' worth of renewals under your belt.

But a strange thing began to happen. I hit a stress tipping point. I began to accept all the adversity I faced. It reminded me of what my father would tell me at times of immense disappointment,

"Man up, you're a Tadevosyan. We are fearless". (Not word for word but this is my best attempt to translate my father's words from Armenian).

I began to notice that there really wasn't enough time for panicking and stressing out. Feeling sorry for myself wasn't helping my situation whatsoever. So, I "manned up," in my father's words and embraced the adversity. So many of these factors were beyond my control. All I could do was ride the wave and handle everything the best I could.

Instead of thinking of all the possible bad things that could happen, I started living in the moment and I noticed I even started counting my blessings. I reminded myself that prayer in times of adversity keeps your focus on the existing good, and not the potential bad.

That weekend, I didn't let myself engage in *any* business activity. I started my Saturday off with a long jog, enjoyed the weekend family plans and reset myself completely for the work week.

When Monday came, I was in a very positive and focused mood. I began the day by making a schedule that included studying for the mortgage exam, team meetings, payroll, tracking, construction business management and everything else I needed to get sorted out. Nothing had changed; but for some reason, I did not feel as overwhelmed. I realized that I could go from very negative, stressed and scared, to positive and motivated just by taking things one step at a time.

I also realized that it didn't *need* to take a few days. I could have made the switch to thinking positively instantly. But managing stress was still new to me. I thought about what changed. I took mental notes of how I went from a bad to a good state of mind and realized that the change, was mainly due to a shift in perspective. I learned adversity was a natural part of life that was there to teach me and make me stronger. This attitude change made it much easier to accept a reality that had the potential to destroy my enthusiasm and creativity. But I could not afford to be weak; my family and loved ones were depending on me.

With a better mindset, I attacked all the things on my to-do list much more effectively. After all, the adversity was behind me. I was able to appreciate the fact that it's not life's conditions that dictate how I feel, but my mindset. Ever since, I *choose* how I feel towards adversity. I discovered that positive thinking is the most powerful weapon, and began to build a capacity to hold it, and to use it efficiently.

SO WHY DON'T WE ALL CARRY THIS WEAPON?

Well, one reason is that people don't like to do hard things. A lot of people prefer the easy way out. Changing your mindset requires some amount of discomfort, discipline, hard work, dedication and time. First you need to get strong enough to pick up this "positivity" weapon and it requires a lot of strength to carry.

For example, when you begin a new exercise program, you start with small reps, small steps, and low weight. Then, more steps and over time, results follow. Being aware is the first step. When you know you're thinking positively or negatively, you can immediately recognize what you are doing. Unless you are conscious of what you are feeding your mind, you will not act to reverse the negative effect.

SMILE 'TILL YOU MAKE IT

There is a well-known study done by Strack, Martin and Strepper in 1988 on handling stress[1]. During their research, one group of participants would bite on a pen in their mouths. The other control group had nothing in their mouths. The purpose of the pen was to force the participant's faces to use the same group of muscles we use when smiling. The study put both groups under similar stressful situations - and the group holding the pens handled the stress much more effectively. They recovered more quickly, and didn't let stress influence how they felt as much.

The conclusion?

Even when you force yourself to smile, the outcome is positive. If all else fails you can always fake it until you make it; after all, even a fake smile can turn into a real one as long as you're using the right muscles.

Being positive and focusing on the good does not mean *ignoring* the bad. Preventative care is only effective when you know both sides of what you are preventing. You want to remain aware of and do a lot of the good; but you also have to know the bad so you can avoid it with good preventative care. In the next chapter I will focus on breaking down the standard bad that none of us are immune to -- to help you develop a better awareness of your blind spots.

To access more tools and resources from Hayk, visit: www.haykt. org/mindset-resources

CHAPTER SIX
SELF-CONTROL OF HEALTHY THOUGHTS

Goals of This Chapter:

- Understand how to avoid the Seven Deadly Sins to maintain healthy thoughts
- Learn how to deal with difficult people
- Avoid relationships that lead to failure
- Understand that issues are disguised tests of your ability to handle basic perspective change

THE 7 DEADLY SINS

Pretty much all categories of new thought, self-help, psychological, motivational, relationship type books --even the Holy Bible -- talk about sins. In particular, the seven deadly sins. According to the Bible, the seven deadly sins are: pride, envy, anger, laziness, covetousness, gluttony and lust.

I have found *pride,* to be the biggest relationship killer of all of these; perhaps it's mentioned first because it's the most dangerous.

Regardless of your religious beliefs, allowing these "sins" into your life and ignoring their adverse impact has the potential to destroy your connection to your authentic self.

While there are some standard explanations of these seven traits, the following definitions are based on my own experiences and observations.

1. PRIDE

This is an ego driven personality trait, usually the result of fear. Fear, is always a losing proposition, creating self-doubt every time. Pride creates a feeling of self-entitlement. People who display pride feel that their "place" is and should remain above others. In order to preserve their self-proclaimed status, they don't practice humility, or attempt to lift others up for fear they may usurp their position. The more modest and humble you are, the lighter you feel as well. A feeling of sincere modesty helps you float high. But pride is heavy; it will only weigh you down.

Do you know anyone that always boasts about their accomplishments? Most likely, he or she also has difficulty uplifting and recognizing others. That individual may also have difficulty making friends. They tend to make others feel inferior and intimidated, and no one likes being put down. Unfortunately, the feeling of inadequacy just compounds -- and their tendencies work against them. They believe that to attract people, they need to boast more and impress others -- which has the exact opposite effect of pushing people away even further.

WHAT IT LOOKS LIKE TO BE PRIDE-FREE

Most of us have looked up to someone at some point. I volunteered to do treasury work for my community and established a good relationship with one of the board members in doing so.

His name is Levon. At first, I knew nothing about Levon, except that he seemed like a very straightforward and honest man. I always noticed he showed up early to our meetings and events. He greeted everyone, was always positive, smiling, serving, and running around helping.

He would stay late to help clean up after church and was usually the first one there. My proud side made excuses as to why he was so good to others - and why it was okay that I wasn't going above and beyond like he did. I assumed he must have nothing else going on outside the community, which is why he was so into this volunteer work.

I thought, he must be a single, bored guy, with no job or family, and all the time in the world. Me, on the other hand - a father of a newborn, busy businessman and at the time I was training for my first full marathon -- had no time to be *that* involved (or so I thought). I showed up occasionally, skipped a few meetings here and there and did what I thought I could, with everything else I had going on.

But as I got to know Levon Esibov over time, I learned that he wasn't just one of the most successful people of my community. He didn't just have a wife and two kids, he was a high-level supervisor, leading a team of engineers for a very large corporation and plenty of other commitments outside of our community. But, he never bragged about all the work he did, or any other accomplishments, including completing his PhD while working. He was a great example of humility -- and the only pride he displayed was pride in helping others, which in my opinion was a huge factor in his success in and outside of work.

2. ENVY

Jealousy is a parasite -- a growing bacteria that, once inside your body, not only infects *you*, but everyone and everything around you. When you start comparing yourself to others, you lose one of the biggest gifts in life, the ability to realize your true potential and grow. Envy makes people negative and judgmental, and fosters an unhealthy competitive mind. They become willing to cut corners just to beat the competition. Jealousy puts all four factors of true success -- Family, Fitness, Finances and Friendships -- at risk. If you're focused on comparing yourself to others, you'll never achieve the goals you set, in these four areas.

When you start neglecting one or more of the four factors, parts of your life start to fall apart. If one or more areas of your life are out of balance, you risk losing your health, family, career and friends altogether. It can be hard to avoid comparing yourself to others - but one tactic is to compliment them for their achievements instead. Be genuinely happy for others, and willing to help. The power of giving is much more powerful than defeating others, taking from others, or cutting corners. Never think anyone is better than you, and never think you are better than anyone. Don't do things based on pleasing or impressing others-just do things *for* others. Meanwhile, always give your best towards your own self and make sure that you are healthy and happy. The action of giving and helping goes from a practice to becoming part of who you are, not what you want. The compounding law of attraction will find a way to pay you back.

Speaking of Envy, I noticed something very interesting after I got married and started a family. I learned that I was oblivious to the impression I was making on others. My father did a good job teaching me focused hard work growing up. He taught me to always give my best at what I could and live one day at a time. So when I discovered my next milestone in life, I would focus on that one pillar immensely. After satisfying my business milestone I discovered wanting a family - so I focused on building a family.

. . .

Unfortunately, those I had once referred to as my peers became people who wished for my failure. We no longer had lighthearted pleasant conversations where we shared stories of success, instead we were competing. Often I would feel like the boring family man with nothing exciting to share from my weekend. My weekends consisted of spending time with my family, taking the kids out to the park, or getting a sitter and taking my wife out on a date. Nothing too exciting to share with someone that partied all weekend and had wild pictures all over social media. I could see their never-ending desperate need to satisfy an endless satisfaction, was killing our group.

Envy had blinded them. They needed to prove to others that they were more exciting, progressive, better and more capable of having a good time, than the boring ones who settle in balance like I did. I understood them clearly, because I use to be that guy. Fortunately, I didn't stay in that phase long. In a way I felt bad for them. I felt put down in many cases from their remarks, because I was not the same Hayk they were used to. I was under the impression that we are built to change, adapt and get better, not to relive the same weekend over and over again. I sensed jealousy towards how happy I was with my *simple life,* versus wanting the *compli! cated shiny coin* addiction they had developed. I felt uncomfortable being around them. I felt if I didn't have something to boast about every time we interacted, I would no longer belong. Over time it got really awkward to maintain these relationships, so we stopped interacting with each other completely. Although envy has little to do with people growing apart as that's part of different choices we make in life - envy was what killed these relationships I'm talking about.

While my relationship with good friends, health, family and finances all improved as the years went by, everything these people worked for fell apart. I heard that some got divorced or moved to another state for a new venture that never worked out. They didn't even return my calls when I tried to check in on them. They were so busy competing and proving themselves, they forgot to make the most of who they truly were. That's the unfortunate thing about jealousy; it forces you to look out the side window so much and so often, that you take your eyes off your own path but fortunately these setbacks can be opportunities to reflect back, learn and improve moving forward. Some of us make more mistakes than others which is why I always say its one of life's greatest hacks to learn from others as we don't live nearly long enough to make all the mistakes and learn from our own history. Although who we are today is the result of our past - what we are capable of becoming is all depended on our ability to learn and grow.

3. ANGER

An unknown but wise individual once said, "Never make any decisions while angry, nor any commitments while happy." Anger causes short-sightedness, impulsiveness and compulsive frustration. An angry mind races to find the most immediate decision with the least amount of effort. Anger doesn't consider the long-term effects, of a thoughtless retort during an argument with someone. Anger will blind you and lead you towards a path of failure and disappointment.

TREAT YOURSELF AND OTHERS WITH THE SAME COMPASSION YOU WOULD SHOW A CHILD

When my two-year-old son is throwing a fit, I sometimes get frustrated and raise my voice. It's a common scenario for a parent of a young child - but it's not a pleasant one. When I see tears form in my son's eyes, it's just too adorable for me to look at - and I can't help but smile. As we know from the study cited earlier, smiling causes happiness that will usually cause a quick change of heart. I pick my son up, and hug and kiss him. More often than not, my anger is immediately replaced with compassion.

It was a huge eye opener for me to remember my interactions with my son, during my daily interactions with people -- and a very easy and effective way to improve my income and relationships. It's basically treating yourself and other adults with the same love and compassion as you would for a child. It can be the difference between a good or bad day, week, month, year and life. When you think about it, most adults still have child-like tendencies and compassion will go a long way with most.

If someone cuts you off in traffic, you usually get frustrated, right? This can lead to cursing, honking, fingers flying everywhere and anger that stays with you for the rest of the day. This frustration eventually affects others who depend on your attention. It can be a stretch, but imagine that the person who cut you off has a sick child in the backseat and is rushing to the hospital, or some other emergency. You can feel good about giving them space so they can get ahead of you, instead of being infuriated. This switch to compassion will remain with you for the rest of the day, as well and affect others around you -- but now in a very *positive* way.

Joy and happiness are the opposite of anger and frustration. They slow you down, and make you smile, which causes your brain to produce feel-good endorphins. Your heart stops racing and you breathe more easily. You start developing a long-term vision of things, rather than reacting in haste. You slow things down and consider your actions and their consequences.

Picture a man sitting and reading a newspaper in his seat on a train. There is a father with three very loud and obnoxious children sitting in the same section. The oldest child is crying, and the daughter is running around with the youngest son. They keep on interrupting the man with screams and running into the man's newspaper.

Eventually the man gets angry and yells, "Can you please get your kids under control! I can't focus here. They keep running into me and interrupting my reading."

The father takes a deep breath and replies, "I'm really sorry about that. We had a long couple of days at the hospital and are now finally on our way home. The kids just lost their mother, and I lost my wife. We watched her die. Again, I'm so sorry; the kids are not taking the loss of their mother well and neither am I."

The man with the newspaper sits back down, speechless for a few moments. He apologizes to the family and encourages them to be as loud as they need to be. He even starts talking to the kids and doing his best to help them feel better. You truly never know another person's mindset, situation, or what they've been dealt. It can be hard to keep this in mind, but it can also be incredibly helpful.

4. LAZINESS

Succeeding in all Four Factors requires you to expend a certain amount of energy. If you don't maintain good health, you will be out of shape and ill. If you stop spending time with friends, you'll be lonely. If you don't take care of your family, they will struggle. If you don't stay hard-working and motivated, you will get fired from your job or your business will fall apart with time.

So why don't all people have good health, money, friends and families? Because we are lazy. There are many reasons for our laziness. Lack of will, feeling helpless, feeling like you don't belong or feeling like you cannot make a meaningful contribution. Absence of motivation usually results from the fact that people don't like to leave their comfort zones - a tendency that causes "in-the-box" thinking. Remember what we learned in Chapter One, it's a survival instinct to be comfortable.

IN- VERSUS OUTSIDE-THE-BOX THINKERS

I recently saw this illustration of kids sitting in a classroom with creative thought bubbles over their heads. The teacher with standard box-shaped thoughts is cutting the children's circular thought edges and shaping them into boxes. The message was clear, people that think inside the box discourage "creative outside-the-box" thinkers.

Inside-the-box thinkers call motivated, imaginative thinkers aggressive, too goal-oriented, and unreasonable. They like to do things, "the way they've always been done". Their way of being has become so comfortable that they see any potential change as dangerous. Our collective comfort zones discourage courageous actions. A feeling of safety is not necessarily the right feeling, it's a branch of laziness that we need to understand better.

The opposite of laziness is hard-work. Hard-work brings income, buys you time to spend with loved ones, keep a healthy body and diet, gives you the ability to donate, volunteer, help others and influence your community. Feeling safe, avoiding risk, maintaining the status-quo, and protecting our comfort zones usually keeps us from achieving more in life. You don't want to be carelessly risking everything at all times. But doing so in carefully considered situations, unlocks opportunities.

WHAT SEPARATES BALANCED SUCCESSFUL PEOPLE FROM THE UNBALANCED SUCCESSFUL?

Why is it that balanced, successful people tend to have more free time, set boundaries for work, have time to spend with family, and still maintain very healthy lifestyles? Meanwhile, the unbalanced successful individuals slave away sixty hours per week, just to maintain their lavish lifestyle. They need as many vacations as they can afford, just to recover from the grind.

The first group made a choice at one point in their lives to either,

a) Stay comfortable and take the safe road ladder, gradually climbing their way up to slow success, or

b) Risk their comfort, work hard and live with the consequences. I know of a lot of extremely intelligent and capable people that *could* start their own consulting firms, commit to a long overdue health goal, start a family or take over a small business.

If they were willing to take the risk, they could make a significant impact on others and their own future. Unfortunately, many of these people are too comfortable with their routines, salary, employer benefits, schedule, lifestyle and their slow growth. They do not want to take the temporary uncomfortable exit off their smooth road, to explore their potential.

Life is never about making bad or wrong decisions, it's about not taking the actions when we had the chance. One of my biggest fears is regretting *in-decisions or in-actions* when I get older and look back on my life. I want to know that when I had the chance to, I took a risk -- even if I failed. I won't regret the lessons I learned, but I know I'd always regret not having the courage to act.

5. COVETOUSNESS

We've already spoken a bit about how an unhealthy competitive spirit is an internal killer of your harmony. There will always be someone that has something that you don't, whether it's a shiny toy, physical feature, or even a personality trait. Many of these are, things money can't buy, efforts can't achieve, and studying cannot develop.

So why would we want something that belongs to someone else if we know we cannot - or in some cases, should not have? Our desire to obtain what we *perceive* to be what we want, can be so strong, it can confuse your priorities and cause mental changes that lead you to adverse consequences. This is when the ability to differentiate wants from needs becomes extremely difficult.

I knew of a younger guy who really wanted to obtain his dream car. Once he secured his first decent paying job, he immediately financed the very car he wanted. In many ways he was unfulfilled, so he brainwashed himself to think that fulfillment would come from driving the same car as the people he admired. He assumed the car would help him feel and be more like the people he admired. It wasn't truly the car he wanted. He wanted his mentors' mindset, but he was unaware of that.

The actual purchase of the car pushed him much further from the very people he admired as the car purchase caused a domino effect of mindset change that lead to more poor decisions. This mindset of material possession, impressing others, keeping up with the Joneses will compound steering you off your path down the wrong lane. His decisions soon lured him into the wrong circle and over time he started drinking, partying and resorted to heavy drugs. Not even a year after buying the car, he unfortunately passed away in a car accident.

. . .

This story taught me a huge lesson in my life. There are certain things that do not belong to us, such as other people's conditions or materials. We have to be very clear what we want, and often it's not what others possess, it's their mindset. If I admire someone and want to be more like them, it doesn't mean dressing more like them, driving the same car as them, or living in a fancy home like them. It means going through their life lessons, reading books they read, and becoming more positive, like they are.

If all we focus on is obtaining "things," we miss the most valuable part of what they represent: mindset.

Eventually a covetous mind causes people to become selfish takers. We do less for others over time until we become only about pleasing ourselves with stuff. We end up mostly hurting ourselves, with this addiction to acquisition.

6. GLUTTONY

Imagine feeling like you never have enough and never being satisfied with what you have. This is Gluttony. When you have this addiction, you concentrate on what you lack and develop a thirst for more. If you feel that you never get enough food, you overindulge, leading to obesity and illness. If you always want more money, you overwork, which causes stress and can also lead to illness. If you exercise too much, this leads to physical exhaustion and fatigue which also causes illness. Feelings of not enough "thrill" can lead you to seek that adrenaline rush and sometimes resort to controlled substances, which also causes illness.

This feeling of never having enough keeps you "always wanting" more, to the point where you don't know *what* you want. You lose a sense of satisfaction, and get caught up in impressing others. You become fixated with competition which leads to pride, envy and anger. Some of these traits can be good for you in moderation, such as being competitive, exercising, working hard, or concentrating on your social life. But when done excessively, the benefit goes away, causing the opposite effect, from what you expected initially.

7. LUST

In my home language, Armenian, the word for lust is *shnanal*, which translates to being dog-like. It's usually not good to be compared to an animal, and that's the case with this sin. Lust is uncontrolled or illicit sexual desire or appetite. It isn't necessarily the act of *doing*, but the mere desire is the sin.

Energy provider company E.ON conducted research where they polled 2,000 British men and women and uncovered the top factors that can make or break a romance.

People were asked what qualities they'd prefer most in a partner. They gave answers of looks, loyalty, honesty, romance, humor, trust and loyalty. Lust is, and engenders the absolute opposite of any kind of trust or loyalty which were the two leading factors couples looked for as result of this research, I know these two are most important to me.

Lust becomes a habit. If you don't intentionally avoid lustful thoughts, they will find a way to occupy and spread in your mind like a virus, and leave you with a lasting dissatisfaction in a relationship. Although lustful thoughts and sexual desires are biological and normal in a relationship, the problem occurs when partners intentionally start having these thoughts about others and don't think of them as issues to their relationship.

All sins are connected, and have a way of complementing each other. Lust can come from gluttony, the state of not having enough or not being stable with what you have. First you start lusting with your thoughts, then eyes, followed by lusting with your body. Both forms of lust kill the laws of mind and body discipline, all the things you worked so hard for.

It is human nature to wonder and be curious. If you are an outgoing, friendly and confident person, you will naturally look at others regardless of gender, purely out of curiosity. You can however, control where your thoughts lead. There is a fine line between looking at someone out of curiosity and lust. Loyalty is mandatory to any relationship and just like any other strength, it takes awareness, practice and time. If you want to strengthen your mind and attain more discipline, this is a great place to start. A strong mind in one area, translates to strength in the next chapter of overcoming difficulties.

We are all guilty of sin. It's simply the result of being human. When sinful thoughts or tendencies creep into your life, understand that it's normal. What matters is how you *act* and handle undesirable thoughts. Asking for forgiveness is a huge part of overcoming sin, but often people confuse why, they are asking for forgiveness. I ask in my prayers, and I know of many people who do the same, for forgiveness of self. The word *forgive* breaks down into two parts, *for* and *give*. It's *for* you to *give* away the poison you have within you, so you can increase the capacity you have for the exact opposite of sin.

So why is it important to avoid sin? Because all sins are a direct result of a lack of discipline.

-*Pride* is the lack of discipline in *humility*
-*Envy* is the lack of discipline in *competition*
-*Anger* is the lack of discipline in *harmony*
-*Laziness* is the lack of discipline in *motivation*
-*Covetousness* is the lack of discipline in *generosity*
-*Gluttony* is the lack of discipline in *satisfaction*
-*Lust* is the lack of discipline in *loyalty*

The more you practice abstinence of sin, the stronger your discipline will become. Often I've seen people put on an act for others on how good and disciplined they are. But you cannot lie to the most important person in your life, yourself.

Yes, others may only see the good side of you, and as satisfying as that might seem while in the company of others, you spend more time in your head than with any other person. Discipline is at its strongest, when you self-reflect and see exactly what you want others to see in you. So whatever it is you want others to see in you, make sure it coincides with what you see in the mirror first.

To access more tools and resources from Hayk, visit: www.haykt. org/mindset-resources

CHAPTER SEVEN
SELF-IMPROVEMENT WHILE PRACTICING SELF-COMPASSION

(AKA HOW TO MAINTAIN YOUR SANITY!)

Goals of This Chapter:

- Understand the difference between improvement and competition
- Learn why adversity is an unavoidable opportunity to get better
- Learn how to take the best action for self-development
- Recognize when your motives are set by other people's conditions and expectations
- Recognize the signs of Unhealthy Competitive Syndrome - UCS
- Determine how to use Healthy Competitive Syndrome - HCS to your advantage
- Understand the importance of practicing Self-Compassion

UCS - UNHEALTHY COMPETITIVE SYNDROME (COMPETING AGAINST OTHERS)

Have you ever been in a situation where "competing" against another person made you lose sleep, made your heart rate go up, and made it so that your competition was pretty much the only thing you could think about?

I was like that once. I had friends like that and still have friends like that today. I call this way of thinking, Unhealthy Competitive Syndrome. It's a form of mental blindness that can affect your wisdom and even your health. Usually, you're the one who needs to recognize it in yourself for it to improve. UCS comes from the initial illusion of wanting to get better in some way, which unknowingly can lead to getting worse. It's common among athletes, career-driven individuals and those that determine their success based on a bar that another individual, usually someone who has circumstances and experiences that differ from yours, has set. The default is to unknowingly mimic them and desire their condition, without knowing, it can be the other way around. They may actually be admiring and mimicking you, all along.

Everyone has or seeks to find a purpose in life. We all want to be great at something. Unfortunately, many of us base our "great' on how other people are doing. We need to understand that we cannot fully come into our own, if we're focusing more on others than ourselves. (i.e., "I'll never be as fit as that other person, so I might as well stop trying.").

EXAMPLE OF UNHEALTHY COMPETITIVE SYNDROME IN ACTION

In my teens, I joined a company to work as a vendor sales producer. Just like any company, this one had its top-producers, which of course management liked to point out and recognize at every possible opportunity. These were ideal examples of what the 'newbies' and average producers needed to become.

It all "looked" great. These people were attractive, very sharp, charismatic and very likable, which all added up to great sales numbers. They also got to the point where no matter what it took, they were unwilling to give up the spotlight. With so much attention and the rewards that followed, these individuals fell victim to Unhealthy Competitive Syndrome.

Losing momentum and falling off the top of the scoreboard was not an option for these individuals, regardless of any other important thing they had to give up, in life. I did very well in my first year. I even set a couple of record-breaking sales. That put me squarely in the middle of what our upper-management called "friendly competition," even though there was *nothing* friendly or healthy about it.

When I ran into the other producers at conferences and meetings, I immediately felt attacked, singled out and interrogated. In one seminar, I received an onstage commendation. A lot of kind-hearted people gave me compliments and good pep talks, especially the management from my team. However, a few people did not react well to me at all. Remarks like "good job newbie - you must be putting in a lot of hours".

"How's your personal life doing, if I was young and single I would be doing more than you."

All with a condescending tone which left a sour taste in my mouth. Those were the same people who had sacrificed their lives, just for the spotlight. At first, I was confused as to why they wanted to put me down. But it made sense later as I began to understand the Unhealthy Competitive Syndrome better.

After this particular seminar, I was hanging out at a bar where others from the meeting were grabbing drinks. Members of the management team and many of the producers were genuinely nice to me. Some of my "friendly competition" asked if it was okay to "pick my brain" about my practice. These didn't feel like friendly advice sessions. They felt more like interrogations. I wondered if they were hoping to catch me doing something unethical so they could report me to human resources and get me fired.

Over the years, I noticed some of the so-called "top producers" disappear due to bending too many company rules. They had to be fired for their behavior by the same management members that were patting them on their backs, and motivating them to produce more at any cost.

When a person is motivated by fame and attention, Unhealthy Competitive Syndrome takes hold much more easily. UCS can prompt people to bend rules of the law, of a company or rules of God, to obtain a temporary benefit. UCS is more of a "condition" (i.e, a syndrome) than a personality trait. It's a way someone becomes or acts due to priorities and circumstances, not necessarily the way they naturally are. So if one doesn't reverse their behavior, it's because they don't want to, not because of a genetic predisposition.

During meetings, I could instantly see some of my colleague's production numbers displayed on their facial expressions. If they were having a good month, they'd be in a good mood. Poor production meant a bad mood. They measured their happiness based on numbers and how superior they felt to others. Every conversation was about their performance, and I somehow always ended up receiving coaching and pointers I never asked for. These individuals seemed to need recognition and to give advice at every opportunity. It took me a while to realize that this "advice" was usually a manipulation method to get me to start talking about how and what *I* was doing. The only thing I could tell them was that I was working hard, but they didn't seem to like that answer. I began to feel as though I was being pushed to give up a secret, or the silver bullet I had found. At the time my silver bullet was, blood, sweat, tears and long hours.

Although I was invited to a lot of their gatherings, it was hard for me to make any friends at the organization. I would find excuses not to go, and if I went, I was the first one out the door. I also noticed their only friends were each other, which made me wonder if they had any friends or loved ones *outside* of the company. I eventually saw that many were happiest with the attention they received from the company. It was a lot more exciting than the stable boring life they had, before becoming rock stars. They almost felt famous, and preferred being around people that praised them, to spending time with friends or even family.

In the first year, I witnessed a few divorces and some dramatic weight gain. This was not a way of life I considered to be synonymous with success. Although the company itself was promoting and maintaining a healthy and good culture, it did not fulfill my definition and comfort with what I considered to be financial success. I didn't belong in the spotlight with the "friendly competition" league.

Of course, there were a few times at the start of my career that I lost sight of what was important to me. The Unhealthy Competitive Syndrome had a negative impact on people that mattered, and my health. Thankfully, I caught this early enough to stop myself. It was mostly a matter of common sense. The more I let business goals and competitors into my life, the more I lost control of what was important to me. That's when I realized that common sense and balance are not common in overly competitive people. All they want to do is win - even if they're not sure exactly why.

This was the first time I implemented the F^4 Formula. This was where I learned that the F^4 formula never comes in any specific order. So I started working on what I was lacking the most, first.

-**Family** - At this time in my life, my family was my father, mother, brother and sister. I began to establish a more meaningful relationship with my brother, who is now one of my best friends. I started helping my father with his business. I got married and I made sure I was spending time with my wife and kids. I didn't miss a single doctor's appointment for my boys. I have been to all of their swimming lessons and activities and don't plan to miss any in the future.

-**Fitness** - When I realized I had gained weight, I implemented a better diet and a consistent workout schedule. I got into the best shape of my life, and started running endurance races such as full, marathons, half marathons, spartan races, tough mudders, 5Ks etc.. I got to the point where jogging felt more comfortable than walking. Now I run at least twenty-five miles per week. This didn't just impact my health, it also inspired my friends and employees to take better care of themselves. I was positively rubbing off on them.

- **Finances** - I learned how to multiply my time through my "+1 routine" (which I'll expand on more in Chapter ten) and the 80/20 rule. I started delegating and even eliminating 80% of low-value tasks and focusing on the top 20%, which lead to the next level of business and financial success.

- **Friendship** - I started saying no to time-consuming commitments such as work trips or meeting clients on their terms. I got selective with who I would meet, when it came to business, declined invites to certain events, and started avoiding people who wanted my time for social status. Instead, I began spending more time with friends. Whether it was more basketball games, working out together, snowboarding, lunch breaks or just hanging out on weekends.

I was beginning to see more of the friends who truly mattered in my life. It brought my true friends closer, and got rid of most of the fake friends- the ones who came to me only when they needed something, but were never there for me when I needed them- for good.

If there was a report measuring the balance of my success in family, fitness, finances and friendship, I can proudly say I'm a rock star producer and will be on top of that report for the rest of my life,- with 0% Unhealthy Competitive Syndrome. However, I will be 100% competitive in Healthy Competitive Syndrome to maintain balance and not lose stability by chasing someone else's idea of success.

Think about what you are using to measure your success and happiness. Was it made by someone else for someone else's benefit? Or made by you, for your benefit? This was a huge eye-opener for me; understanding the illusion of happiness versus realizing what my version of happiness was.

HCS - HEALTHY COMPETITIVE SYNDROME (COMPETING AGAINST YOURSELF)

The opposite of Unhealthy Competitive Syndrome is Healthy Competitive Syndrome. Getting rid of UCS helps, but doesn't automatically guarantee that HCS will replace it. You have to work to develop the Healthy Competitive Syndrome. I love using health and fitness examples as they have been a big part of noticeable and measurable results in my life. Eliminating bad food and starting to eat healthy is a good first step. But to take your health to the next level, you have to implement exercise - i.e., Healthy Competitive Syndrome. This is when you start practicing and developing a balance. When you stop competing with others. However, a lot of times, we don't know who or what the competition is.

Let's say you envy the fact that someone you know makes a million dollars per year. You sacrifice all you can, your health, family, friends, everything else you enjoy, and achieve a two-million-dollar income. You might have beaten the so-called competition, but you lost everything else.

So, how is this success?

A true balance of the 4F's is the result of Healthy Competitive Syndrome. Of course, if you're falling short in one of these four areas, you should sacrifice other time consuming activities to re-achieve balance. If you are very poor because you spend too much time on fitness or with friends or family you should sacrifice some of that time, to achieve financial stability. If you lack social support, it might be because you work too much, so you might consider spending less time at work, to spend more time with friends. Once you get a feel of what you need with all four, then you can start balancing things out. We are the happiest when we are present. Achieving balance helps us become more PRESENT, by utilizing the proper application of our competitive spirit.

How do we differentiate today's reality versus yesterday or tomorrow's illusion? Here are a few simple techniques.

REALITY VERSUS ILLUSION

How can you tell the difference between reality and illusion? If you can manipulate the thought-idea-belief, then it's an illusion. Reality does not change, it's consistent. If, for example, your circle of friends, is extremely negative, it doesn't matter how you think of them, the reality is they will be negative and skeptical no matter what.

FEAR AS A SOURCE OF ILLUSION

Let's examine a common source of illusion, fear. I understand people have phobias and fears. I have some of these myself. I have

Acrophobia (Fear of heights), but sometimes I can trick my mind into being okay with heights. The key was positive, courageous self-talk and thinking of the worst case scenario as well as odds of that actually happening to me. I have learned to accept that this fear is an illusion that doesn't have to define me. Over the years I have learned to manage my fear of heights and to be okay with looking down from balconies, windows and glass elevators.

USING LOVE TO OVERCOME FEAR

If you remove fear, what are you left with? I've heard a lot of answers for this. For example, "the absence of fear is courage", or "courage is not the absence of fear, but mastering fear."

One of my favorite quotes about this subject is by Mark Twain

"Courage is resistance to fear, mastery of fear, not absence of fear."

I've discovered, the opposite of fear is love. Love is courage, energy, positivity, success and happiness. To avoid fear, we should work towards loving more. Recall the Law of Occupancy from Chapter five. The empty space is always filled by the opposite. So if your positive thoughts do not fill 100% of your mind, the negative will always take up the difference. Often, when it's difficult to eliminate one thing like *fear*, it's easier to get consumed by its exact opposite, *love*. I don't just mean loving family members and those closest to you, you have to love them. This is unconditional love for all. Accepting people and being genuinely interested in being there for people regardless of condition or closeness. It's a state of mind to be loving no matter what, not a per-individual base commitment.

ENJOY THE JOURNEY & LIVE WITHOUT REGRETS

Fear has a way of eliminating action from our lives and keeping us slaves to our comfort zone. Often, the mere thought of failure prompts so much fear into us, that we simply don't take any action at all. Most people have heard the phrase, "It's not about the destination, it's about the journey?"

When was the last time you wanted to watch a good movie, just to skip to the ending and watch the last ten minutes? Odds are, you wanted to enjoy the storyline. Our focus on challenging results - and failing to consider that we might enjoy our path in getting those results, can prevent us from doing some amazing things.

What have you regretted and what will you regret?

I bet if you think back, you have more regrets about the things that you wanted but did not do, versus any failures you experienced. Remember what we've already discussed: failures are lessons that help us grow.

I can proudly say I feel as though I've never failed, since I've always learned a valuable lesson from all the things that did not end, in the way I had initially wanted them to. However, I do have some regrets about not doing something that I should have, because I focused too much on my safety, versus the potential gain. I fear that I have passed on a lot of good opportunities by being too fearful of loss at times when I needed to be more courageous, and loving.

A peer of mine who I will keep anonymous for this example, approached me five years ago with a business proposition. He wanted a loan of fifty-thousand dollars and my involvement, and in return I'd own a percentage of his start-up business. If I had the guts to commit, which seemed like the right thing at the time, that fifty-thousand dollars would have translated into millions of dollars over the last five years but I didn't do it.

Missed opportunities from our past are forms of failure. However, as I've stated before, we can't live in the past. I practice what I preach and learn valuable lessons from my missed opportunities. If fear is the only reason why I don't commit to a smart decision, then I have to think with love.

The other day a friend of mine corrected my grammar when he overheard me say to someone on the phone, "What was your name again?"

He pointed out that someone's name does not change. The proper way to ask is, "What *is* your name again?" I felt a little embarrassed knowing that I've been saying this wrong for years, but I got a lesson in the proper way of asking someone to repeat their name. The big picture lesson here is to never be offended when corrected, but to always be accepting of pointers and advice. It's hard to live in regret and anger when you're open-minded towards learning.

DO YOURSELF A FAVOR: FORGIVE EVERYONE AND EVERYTHING

Another important element of courage is being able to forgive others. Some of us can build up resentment and feel that things are unfair. We wonder, "Why can't I find a better job? Why am I so unlucky? Why don't I have what other people have? I'm unhealthy. I am unattractive. Why don't I have better friends? Why am I not motivated? Why am I broke?" - and countless other questions and gripes. Building up negative thoughts and blaming others engenders not just a negative attitude, but also fuels your fear. That's why it's critical to be able to forgive.

According to the greater good educational website, "Psychologists generally define forgiveness as a conscious, deliberate decision to release feelings of resentment or vengeance toward a person or group who has harmed you, regardless of whether they actually deserve your forgiveness."

The above definition is my favorite due to the word *conscious*. While some forgive to have someone else *owe* them one, those who do it consciously are deliberately doing it for the highest good. They don't have ulterior motives. They forgive because they know it's the right thing to do.

When was the last time you *consciously* forgave someone? Remember, anger is a killer of love and creativity. Why do we keep this poison within us that compounds and affects everything around us? People hesitate to forgive. Some people worry that forgiving gives the other party the green light to do whatever they did again. Or, they think that what they did, was not wrong. But forgiving someone does not make the wrong-doing okay. Forgiving is settling the anger within *you*. It's the release of poison that prevents happiness, courage, positivity and all other love generating energy. Forgiveness is always more of a gift to yourself, than to the person you're forgiving.

Think about the word and memorize it. FOR-GIVE. Who are you doing it FOR? Not for others, but for yourself. What are you doing? You are GIVING the poison away. You are giving up hate, vengeance and fear, which will be replaced with love. When you are consumed by love, happiness and positivity follow. Remember, we are all equal. If one person is capable, then we are all capable. If a universal law applies to one, it applies to all.

The act of forgiving someone is both an act of compassion for the other person and an act of self-compassion. To forgive *yourself* is often an even harder task, and an even greater act of self-compassion.

SELF-COMPASSION

The Golden Rule says to treat others the way you want to be treated. It doesn't offer any caveats about how to treat the people that are consistently bad towards you, or who negatively impact who you are becoming. If someone judges you enough times either by putting you down or by uplifting you, after a while you will believe them. That's why both positive and negative affirmations are both so powerful.

Over time we become products of our own environment. When a person is insecure and hard on themselves, because of whatever issues they've faced in their lives, they become less forgiving and less kind to themselves. They judge themselves and isolate themselves from the rest of the world. They might even start thinking they are unique to adversity, begin to blame themselves for things that are out of their control and continue a loveless life.

Self-compassion is critical for confidence and personal security. It's not something you can just create, especially if it's been chipped away over the years. It can take time and practice to bring back. The easiest way I found to practice self-compassion, is through your circle of friends and family. Reflect on the type of people that surround you, the ones that give you confidence, and are genuinely positive and supportive of you. Then, start spending more time with those people. Their way of living will be crucial towards your practice of bringing more compassion into your life.

You will need to develop a more consistent belief system. Bad things don't happen to you because you are dumb, unprepared, not made for happiness or you're unable to be lucky. They happen because they're part of life, and that's not your fault. Adversity is an unavoidable opportunity to get better. So instead of blaming ourselves or others, we need to train our minds to be more accepting of what comes into our lives. Criticizing yourself only causes more fear and regret, which leads less room for courage and compassion. Practicing to love yourself can be even more important than loving others. If you don't love yourself, you will not have the capacity to love others.

Success will throw obstacles your way to test if you are ready. The people who are ready are the ones that stick to their commitments, and develop passion towards improvement. This also requires committing to self-compassion. This is a good place to apply the C.A.A.R. Formula from Chapter three.

You have to be **clear** on what's missing before taking **action**. Then, when you take action, you will have the **activity,** which is the routine and the habit of sticking to your commitment. Eventually, this will bring you the **results** you were seeking. Re-read chapter three and start putting a plan together to invest more into yourself and to help you work more completely with others. Self-compassion is a crucial component of the F^4 formula, since the two of the F's - *Family* and *Friends*, require you to show love towards others. It's impossible to have good relationships with others, when you don't have one with yourself.

To access more tools and resources from Hayk, visit: www.haykt. org/mindset-resources

CHAPTER EIGHT
SELF-ATTRACTION

ATTRACT THE RIGHT PEOPLE AND THE RIGHT ADVICE

We are the product of our society. Fortunately, we have the right to choose who we surround ourselves with.

Goals of This Chapter:

- Know how to utilize your relationships to their fullest
- Discern who is good for you and who is bad for you
- Know who to avoid in order to fully be yourself
- Know who to approach for advice, and when
- Understand why certain advice and implementation of advice works or fails

Your relationships with others is important to balancing family, friends, fitness and finances. Your relationship with your spouse and children is your water. Your work peers are your bread and butter. Your fitness is your vitamins, and your friends are your recovery.

A very powerful ingredient in success is the people you

surround yourself with, your relationships. When your peers set a standard or example, it can become a way of doing something that makes its way into your comfort zone. You are the product of your environment. Over time, you tend to surround yourself with the environment you are most comfortable with. This can be good or bad. When things are going well, we don't believe change is required until we encounter difficulty. It feels good to be in a comfort zone when things are going well. However, unless you can duplicate what your "good" is, then what you have is not sustainable and can be taken away by adversity, faster than what it took to obtain it. One important thing to determine is whether the people around you are helping or hindering you.

LIKE ATTRACTS LIKE

You get to choose who you surround yourself with. Absolutely with friends, a little less so with coworkers. However, the most important change that needs to take place is the change within yourself.

I'm very humbled to have gotten to a place in the business world where others reach out to me for coaching. I've been asked about mindset, accountability, work ethic, hiring people, marketing and more. I'll use hiring as an example, since one of the most expensive and challenging parts of running an organization, is finding and keeping good employees.

When I ask other employers what they're looking for, I often hear, "I want motivated, hardworking, focused, determined, driven, positive, coachable and competitive employees!"

This is how I learned to respond:

"Is that who and what *you* are?" Because remember, "YOU NEVER ATTRACT WHO and WHAT YOU WANT. BUT YOU'LL ALWAYS ATTRACT WHO and WHAT YOU ARE."

. . .

Have you ever stepped back and realized what or who you are attracting? Because, they are all an extension of you. Employers can make a bad judgment and hire bad people. Consequently, you fire them. It's both a good and bad thing that we tend to settle for the people that make us most comfortable in business, and in our personal lives. How can you be comfortable with a positive, ambitious, hardworking person when you are negative, scared and lazy? So, instead of ruminating on how hard it is to find good people for your organization, self-reflect on what might be bringing the bad candidates. Same goes for your friends.

To access more tools and resources from Hayk, visit: www.haykt. org/mindset-resources

HOW TO ATTRACT THE
RIGHT PEOPLE INTO
YOUR LIFE

Dale Carnegie wrote a very famous book called, *How to Make Friends and In! uence People*[1]. It was one of the first self-help books published to have sold millions of copies. I highly recommend this book, as it covers the "why" behind being genuinely interested in people is important. The book explains why it's import to smile, and why positivity is the key to connecting and developing the relationships we seek.

It's contagious to be positive, but it can be very hard to start.

It is possible to practice positivity, smiling, good habits, and good decision making. Did you know, on a biochemical level you can literally fake a smile, which will trick your mind into thinking you are happy? Smiling can release endorphins and serotonin into your brain, causing a happy feeling. This will then turn your fake smile into a genuine one. Start to practice positivity by starting your day off with smiling in the mirror, as well as greeting and complimenting strangers with a smile. With time, you will become more positive. That happiness can feel so good, that you can get addicted. Your body and mind work on the same scale of consistent patterns. Sometimes we think we are too different and unique to follow certain rules like smiling, repetitions, routine. But, we need to think again.

I've seen acquaintances having "fun" and "enjoying" life that made fun of me when I had my head down in books and in building my business. They told me that I was taking life too seriously. They wanted me to join them at bars and clubs on weekends. They said I needed to be more spontaneous and not turn down a random invite to a party on a Wednesday night. They tried to persuade me to buy the car I wanted and stop trying to save for a rainy day. They told me I needed to date more and not settle down. To vacation more and work less. When I concentrated on my health, they told me I should eat and drink what I wanted and not care about the way I look and what kind of people I'm attracting into my life. I mistakenly called those acquaintances my friends and quickly learned that this wasn't the case. But when I think back, I realized that the people around me were always a direct reflection of who *I* was at that time.

In my early twenties, all I cared about was going out and partying, so did all my friends. Some friends didn't change and stayed where they were. As time passed, we hung out less and less. As I got older, I surrounded myself with people who had the same values that I did. Attracting the right people can seem like a very slow process, but if you look back one, three, five or ten years ago, it can go by in the blink of an eye. If you aren't careful, you will catch yourself asking how you ended up with the people that you are with, today.

WHEN IN DOUBT ALLOW YOUR LOVE FOR OTHERS TO GUIDE YOU

When we are in doubt, whether to make a hard change in our lives, we often give some thought to how the people we're close to will react. A good friend of mine once said, "I honestly don't care what happens to me based on my actions and my risk, it's the emotional impact on my loved ones that matters the most to me." Knowing that he was not the only person who would be affected by his decisions, kept him safe, even though he was a bit of a troublemaker. It's healthy to think of the ones we influence and mentor before we make a possible life-changing decision.

3 KINDS OF PEOPLE SURROUNDING YOU

There are three kinds of people you surround yourself with:

1. Those that see the positive in you
2. Those that see the negative in you
3. Those that remain neutral

Think of yourself as an atom - you have protons (the positive force), electrons (the negative force), and the neutron (the neutral force.) Each is completely different, but no matter what, we will always be surrounded by them. Unlike an atom, we humans have the ability to control the type of people we allow into our lives, and therefore the amount of positive, negative and neutral forces.

COMMON "ELECTRON" OR NEGATIVE PEOPLE IN YOUR LIFE

The first step is to identify who the electrons are. Below I've listed some common types of electrons, in no particular order. I have developed these personas with nicknames I have for people I am, or have associated with. Odds are, they'll sound familiar to you too.

THE INVOLUNTARY CONSTRUCTIVE CRITIQUE

These are the people who heap unwanted and irrelevant advice on you, and make you feel like your ideas have zero importance. They will highlight the slightest negative possibility. They will put themselves above you and do whatever they can to make you feel as if you are wasting your time, with whatever you are working on. Perhaps it's the boss who you feel you can never please, or even a parent whose expectations you can't seem to live up to.

What to do: If this person is truly a friend of yours and the relationship matters to you, it helps to start your communications with them, using words of affirmation. Find their true strengths and focus on them. Odds are, this person has a great deal of positive attributes. However, they might also have an inferiority complex. One way to neutralize this shortcoming is to genuinely acknowledge and highlight what they're good at. This will neutralize their negative tendencies and make the rest of your interactions less irritating.

The book *The Five Love Languages* by Gary Chapman

²explains extremely well how to deal with certain personality types. For this particular person, words of affirmation is the key. If the relationship is irrelevant to you, then ignore this person and move on. No one needs that kind of negativity, if they can avoid it!

THE CONSISTENT VICTIM NAGGER

The forever victim is plagued with self-pity, and believes that no one else could possibly understand their struggle. They always think they have more on their plate than others, so they never have enough time for others. Things just get worse and worse. In line with the Law of Occupancy, they focus so much on the negative, there is no longer any room for positive thoughts.

What to do: Try to get this person to count their blessings. This can be the difference between them dragging you down or having a positive interaction. Again, if this person is important to you it will require extra effort on your end, but if not, keep them at a distance.

THE WET BLANKET

Automatically pessimistic, they will find negativity in anything. Just like a wet blanket, they will always make you feel uncomfortable and shoot down your ambitions and ideas. They will tell you why optimism is pessimistic, and call themselves "realists." This is the person that does not believe in the greatness that you can achieve, and believes we are all born to be mediocre in health, wealth, family and friendships. Any effort put towards excellence is a waste of time.

What to do: This is an extremely difficult person to deal with. If whatever good they offer doesn't compensate for this personality type, keep them at a distance. It will likely take a great deal of compromise to make this relationship work, and a careful approach to what you share with them.

THE TRAIN

This person loudly and obnoxiously invades your space with force, knocking you down without even realizing it. They lack both self-awareness and self-control. They are and have the latest and greatest news and when they enter the room, the attention must always be on them. You notice the heightened level of excitement, but when you hear them speak, their message has no importance or urgency whatsoever.

What to do: Someone as thoughtless as this person probably doesn't realize the damage they're doing to your friendship, as well as the other relationships they have. You most likely don't have a good relationship with this person to compromise, so the best thing here is to avoid them as they will distract you from your destination.

THE GOSSIP

This person is the rumor spreader, the one that shares secrets just to get a rise out of others, and for their own amusement. Usually this is because they find their own lives dull. This individual usually has a very poor reputation, both at work and in their personal lives, since no one wants to share anything with them. Therefore, this person has difficulty establishing deep relationships.

What to do: There is always a chance to change people. Even if this is a particularly tough cookie, you can tell them what you think, and point out what they're doing with specific examples. If that doesn't change their ways, then avoid them and never share anything that you don't want to go public.

THE OBSESSIVE CONTROLLER

This person always feels their way is the best way and must control all situations, ideas and all outcomes. They are usually stressed out about whatever situation, or person they're trying to control. When they are in control, they are ecstatic. When things are out of their control, they are depressed. Since most things do not go as planned, they are extremely moody individuals. Unfortunately, they never view adversity as opportunity, only as failure.

What to do: If the relationship matters to you, remind this person that things usually *don't* go as planned. Teach them the lessons you learned in this book.

- If you live in the future, you live in fear;
- If you live in the past, you live in regret;
- To be happy, live in the moment".

This person is very much in fear of things not going as planned or has memories of what "could have/ should have/ would have" been. He or she is not necessarily a bad person, but their negative mood can affect you. You can deal with them by managing the conversations. Let them know that it's ok if things are out of control sometimes, and point out the opportunities in adversity. Again, if the relationship is not worth it, save yourself the hassle and avoid them.

BACK STABBER

The name is pretty self-explanatory. You must be careful what you say to or share with a backstabber. Therefore, you can never develop a deep relationship with this person. They usually have no friends and people tend to keep their distance as they fear getting hurt.

What to do: Avoid them; they mean you harm and don't deserve your loyalty.

THE ACTIVE VOLCANO

You're almost afraid to talk to or give any criticism to the active volcano, since they may erupt, out of nowhere. They are unpredictable, unstable, and very volatile. They also have issues developing long-term relationships. You have to watch every single step carefully, which causes you to feel nervous at all times, - and in some cases- even scared.

What to do: The thought of spending time with this person is dreadful, usually you avoid them anyway. You should not feel bad ignoring them. Continue to ignore them until they go away.

THE LIMITLESS ABSORBING SPONGE

The limitless absorbing sponge always wants something from you. "Give me. Give me," is their mantra. They will take no matter what, but will never give. They are self-centered and egotistical. You could also call them black holes, as the gravity these individuals generate is so strong that whatever enters, has no way out. Even the most giving person can become selfish if they spend enough time with the limitless absorbing sponge. When in a very rare occasion this individual actually gives, they will remind you of their "rarest, greatest and kindest act ever," for the rest of your life.

What to do: This person doesn't intentionally want to hurt you. However, they *will* make you feel drained and low on energy. They are big time users and are with you for some kind of benefit. You usually cannot recognize the benefit from spending time with them, as their purpose is to take for personal gain and to never give. The best thing to do here is to avoid them. Truly good friends are givers. If you have a relationship with someone like this, ask yourself whether they spend time with you because you have a genuine relationship, or because they constantly need something.

THE ENEMY

No matter who this person surrounds themselves with, the enemy is always looking for something that they dislike about others. They pinpoint flaws or even make them up, and seem to believe that good people don't exist. It's almost as if the entire world is against them, and they are one of the last few good people left, that no one understands. They have pretty convincing reasons why everyone is bad, which are usually exaggerated and never true. It's tough to establish a friendship with this person. They may be kind to your face, but will describe you to the next person as the enemy.

What to do: Do yourself a favor, end the relationship yourself or they will find a reason to do it themselves.

BECOME AN EXPERT IN HOW YOU ALLOCATE YOUR TIME IN PEOPLE

I have had periods of time when I only noticed the negative in people, even my former self. No one is perfect, of course, but it prompted me to ask the question, "Does the negative outweigh the positive?"

My father told me this several times growing up. He will always be my first mentor, as most fathers are. He said, "Don't focus on the negative in people, otherwise you will be left alone." This was the idea of learning to perfectly love an imperfect person. I always saw my father as a reasonable man with good justifications. Sometimes he pushed people away for what I'd consider good reasons. But sometimes his reasons didn't seem warranted. I learned that he wasn't *too* forgiving, even though he's one of the most loving people I know. People's emotions get in the way of their own advice.

I adopted this trait from my father. Luckily, I learned that it's a weakness and eventually became wary of my pride. I worked on eliminating it and then proving to people that I have none. I developed a genuine interest in getting to know people. I was able to look past certain negative personality traits and would only focus on the positive in all people I met. It didn't take long before I realized, I had on blinders. Although it's great to see the positivity in people, it is not good to avoid the negative.

You want to be forgiving, but that doesn't mean you should keep everyone around you. It's great to be generous, but it doesn't mean you should give to everyone. It's great to be kind, but not everyone deserves your kindness.

I would give to all, forgive anything, and ignore the worst in people.

In the early stages of building my business, I went a little overboard in giving my clients access to me. I shared my cell phone number with all of my clients, and told them to call me at any time. I encouraged them to text and call me, even on the weekends. This worked well for a few months, until I realized that they were indeed doing exactly what I'd asked them to do. I was getting calls late at night, weekends, and holidays. I had no time off. I was getting harassed by abusive clients who'd call multiple times a day. They'd act as though they had an "emergency," meanwhile, their reason for calling was such a small matter, even my newest-inexperienced team members could have helped with it. And of course, the call could have waited until the next day. Because I had given them access to contact me personally at any time, no one would utilize my team. My respectful, kind and understanding clients only called me for *true* emergencies.

. . .

Although I felt harassed, I would always smile, welcome the client's call and take care of them on the spot. Looking back, I realized I was doing disservice to my customers by allowing them such extreme access to me. They treated my cellphone as a convenience to get help on the spot. I had disabled my clients instead of enabling them to use my team. I got to the point where I felt there was nothing I could do. I couldn't turn my cell phone off, because I was afraid I'd lose clients, and I didn't have the guts to ask them to stop calling my phone. This continued for over a year until I finally said, enough is enough. With the support of my business coach Dan Sevier, I decided to cancel that cellphone line. I called my phone company and did just that.

I worried this would cause me to go out of business, and I did lose some clients at this time. But I didn't go out of business. I took the very necessary step of retraining my clients to utilize my team. I told them I would no longer be available on the first call -- and most of the good clients didn't care. A few adjusted slowly, and the bloodsuckers disappeared, which made my life a lot better! Over time, my business started doing even better than before, because I now had the time to focus on what I needed to be doing rather than constantly answering phone calls.

I realized I was doing the same with peers, in short, I was a YES man. I had a difficult time freeing myself from the people who took up a lot of my time and energy. The change I've made in my professional life also clarified my issue of committing to everything in my personal life. I began to properly allocate my time with people, and slowly became comfortable saying NO. Although it sounds contradicting, doing less led to my clients being happier with my business. Less truly is more!

I eventually became very aware of the type of people I allowed into my circle, and who I should let go. I found a balance between being accepting and discerning. I became an expert on how to allocate my time with people through trial and error. I noticed a drastic change in how my relationships appreciated in value, and not just for me. I saw myself becoming a more valued friend to others. Time is the most precious and valuable asset we have. Wasting it in the wrong place, or with the wrong people is much worse than working hard for money and throwing it away. Although the progress I've made has been slow, it's progress that I'm very proud of. My time is now spent with people that push and make me better with every interaction, not the other way around.

COMMON "PROTONS" OR POSITIVE PEOPLE IN YOUR LIFE

Just like the electrons circling us, we're also surrounded by protons. Below are descriptions of traits to look for in the type of people you want to have around, the ones that will make you better and provide help in times of need. These types of people are those with whom I have established great friendships, partnerships, put together good strategies, and made a positive impact in my community. Of course, some people are more than one type. I broke them down individually to describe them better. If you have a deep relationship with someone you love, you can likely assign at least one of the descriptions below to that person.

THE SUNSHINE

This individual is always in a good mood, smiling for seemingly no reason. You rarely hear them complain and they tend to make you feel uncontrollably good. They have a very light personality that never weighs you down, or makes you feel stressed out. You can't help but crave this individual's presence, consciously or unconsciously. You simply like the way you feel around them.

THE VAULT

This individual has strong discipline and has no problems keeping your secrets. You can tell this individual anything you want without any hesitation because they know what is inappropriate to share with others, about your life. They make you feel free, and you're able to get into very deep conversations with them, with no regret or worry about what you've shared. It's very easy to establish a deep friendship with this person. They often know more about you, than anyone else in your life.

THE PROTECTOR

The safe, controlled environment that this person creates for you is incomparable. If you ever get into a fight or trouble, you want this person there. He or she will definitely have your back. When you feel weak, this is the person you want to hold your hand. You feel that this person will get you unstuck when you're stuck, and in many cases fight your battles with you, or even for you. You trust and believe in this person immensely. They are your business partner, your workout buddy, the person who makes you feel the kind of safety that all humans crave.

THE FLASHLIGHT

This is the person you go to for answers because they shine a light on any dark, unexplainable part of your struggle. They will always see opportunity in adversity, and the good in the bad. They make great business partners, as they encourage all of your decisions and commitments. They help you feel smart and capable and bring out great ideas and thoughts. You naturally become better at, and love sharing ideas, business ventures, and new innovations with this person. They will help you see your ideas through to the end, and will only positively contribute to your endeavors.

THE OWL

This individual is both very intelligent and experienced. Their advice might not always be what you want to hear, but it will always be genuine and in your best interest. This is the friend who might be busy, or not as much "fun", but he or she is like a lifeline. They act as a mentor and look out for your best interest. They will give you the pros and cons of your ideas and commitments, and will always be truthful. They usually have a very strong memory, because they listen intently when you and others speak, and are very well spoken. Occasionally, they will need to bring you back down to reality, but they do it in a loving way.

THE RULER

This is the most straightforward person you know. They don't filter anything they say, and while they aren't always wise, they're always truthful. This is the person that will shake you up and raise their voice when you are not hearing the point. They are not negative but can be a little critical. Unlike the wise friend, they will not have a constructive conversation with you. Instead, they'll tell you the first thing that comes to their mind, to keep you out of harm. They might not give you the right advice every time, but they will give you a good perspective. This is the person who should prompt you to get a second opinion, perhaps from your Owl.

THE HEAVY HITTER

This friend supports any thought you have, good or bad. They will encourage and motivate you. They are a huge risk-taker, and are constantly seeking adrenaline. They make some of the best fitness partners, and are your loudest cheerleaders. They support you intensely, but it doesn't necessarily feel genuine. It's always consistently optimistic, and not unique to you. You will have memories of having the most fun with this person, however, they usually have a lot of friends, and not much time for you. Odds are you have a lot of fun, and can enjoy yourself and unwind with them. This person provides a charge when your battery is low, the pump-up you need before a workout, and the motivation before a challenge.

THE INNOVATOR

This person will always remember you, have good intentions, and admire you. You don't spend much time with this person, but you like the way they make you feel. They are always working on their next business or personal venture, and want you to be part of it. This person is very disruptive, so you have to learn to say no to them. There are times you can and should say yes to their carefully planned and thought out ideas. If timed correctly, this person can help you acquire a great amount of financial, health or relationship gain. They only see good in you, and often seek your mentorship in a subtle way. They won't state this desire outright. They look up to you and listen to everything you say, but will never admit it. This person allows you to be a teacher, and get better at what you have already mastered, by showing it to them. You can't help but feel important and valued around this individual.

"NEUTRONS" OR NEUTRAL PEOPLE IN YOUR LIFE

There aren't too many neutrons in our lives. This is the group that is neither good nor bad for you. These are the ones who are more influenced by you, than you are by them. This is the person with whom you might have awkward conversations, and try to avoid interactions. They are not very driven individuals, but they are not negative either. Their passiveness is almost contagious. You never really feel a reason to encourage this relationship or end it, so it's just *there*. The best thing to do with these people is take some sort of action, pull them in, and give them access to your passion, ambitions and enthusiasm. Because they are so easily influenced, they'll end up following someone, even if it's not you. Neutrons need a mentor in their lives. They pay attention to what you say and do, so you have to serve as an example. Push them to discomfort, motivate them and keep them accountable.

It is very common to know one person who embodies more than one of these personality descriptions. You may assign just one negative personality type to someone you know, which is for the best, because as soon as you get to know this person well enough, you realized you didn't like them, and saved yourself a lot of time by ending that relationship. Humans have a tendency to connect emotions and memories to a single experience with another person. After that, he or she is defined by that moment.

Only you can determine based on who you are, who you want to surround yourself with. The first step is to recognize the people you already have in your life so you can decide whether to bring individuals closer, or distance yourself from them.

Now that you have a better idea of the positive traits to look for in people, you can start looking for the same traits in people you hope to seek advice from, or perhaps even in your future mentors. Let's take a look at how to seek out the best advice for yourself, using The Advice Formula.

To access more tools and resources from Hayk, visit: www.haykt. org/mindset-resources

THE ADVICE FORMULA: HOW TO SEEK OUT THE RIGHT ADVICE FOR YOURSELF

"Dumb people don't learn anything. Smart people learn from their mistakes. Geniuses learn from other people's mistakes."
~Albert Einstein.

I have been all three of these when it comes to learning: dumb, smart and a genius. One way to take the genius approach is to seek out mentors, books, articles, or other sources of advice who will share with you the lessons they've learned from their own hard knocks in life. That's one of the main reasons why I wrote this book, to help you learn from my missteps.

We all need to be humble and modest enough to ask for advice. Most people love to give advice. Humans seek recognition, and a desire to guide others in their choices and actions. This can help us feel recognized. It's critical to consider, though, whether we're giving or receiving the right advice, at the right time. Think about the message (i.e., the advice itself), the timing of it, and the person it's coming from, when deciding whether to follow it.

For instance, in my business, and most businesses, hiring and managing a team is a continuous challenge. I would periodically reach out to other entrepreneurs, and ask for their perspective on whatever I was struggling with at the time. Sometimes it would help, and sometimes not. Eventually, I was able to develop a *formula* that taught me the importance and the appropriateness of timing the advice, to my advantage.

(Me + good advice) x Person I don't admire or look up to = no change, no results

(Me + good advice) x Person I admire and look up to = change and positive outcome

It was pretty simple. If I didn't relate to the messenger, I did not see myself implementing their advice. Usually, unsolicited advice is the worst timed. It's usually ego driven advice, that is, advice people give to feel good about themselves that really isn't going to help the person receiving it, in a significant way. These individuals usually lack self-awareness and have no idea they're misleading others. It's uncomfortable to have someone who always looks for reasons to coach you. If you think about it, these tend to be people who don't have too many close friends. If you ever want to help this individual, just call them out on what they're doing. You might shine a light on why they have difficulty establishing deep relationships.

When you admire someone, it usually means you want to be where they are, professionally or personally, so you attempt to mimic them. When a physically fit person gives you welcomed exercise advice, you are much more likely to implement it than identical fitness advice from an out of shape person. This happens because the first individual is experiencing the results that you are seeking. You'll accept advice more readily from the right person, and acceptance is a key to implementation. When you focus more on the journey than the results, the advice becomes easier to implement, and you can get to your goal, one step at a time. If we put this in a formula, it looks like this:

RA + RP = RR.

Right Advice + Right Person = Right Results or positive outcome

When I was in high school, I developed a mentor like relationship with the father of my girlfriend. His name is John Jackson. He was a consultant executive in charge of a business group with a large corporation. I really admired him. He was a great father, husband, healthy, had true friends and was very successful. In fact, he was pretty much everything I wanted to become one day. Although I had been getting all sorts of business advice from a lot of different people, John's guidance really resonated with me. He was the man that educated me on the corporate business environment, professional licensing, grit, long-term commitment, and even referred me to work for a local small business owner that he knew of. When someone you admire steers you in the right direction, it gives you the confidence you need to take action. And that action is the key in heading the right direction, I know it was for me thanks to John.

POSITIVE ROLE MODELS AND MENTORS

When I was 21 and was beginning my business journey, I was very careful in what business to commit to. So I started my research online. I stumbled upon an article about all the "bad" in the same business world I was looking to enter which was the insurance industry. I pretty much found the black hole of all the failed businessmen, complaining about their experiences in the industry. With each blog post I read, I caught myself becoming increasingly disappointed, and almost convinced myself to agree with these people. I felt invincible at 21. I wanted to be the most successful entrepreneur in the world, while also being the best athlete, while one day running for Congress, and helping millions of people. Yet all that positivity was jeopardized in just an hour of ingesting negative information. I had to shake it off, and it took me a few days to recover. I did that by reaching out to my mentors, and some of the best people in the industry, to get positive about the opportunity again. I can't stress the importance of mentorship enough, and not just towards keeping you on the right track, but also towards keeping your friendship tank filled. Your mentors can become your best friends. Having the *right* people in your life at times of ambiguity, is the simple secret towards making the *right* choices towards clarity.

To access more tools and resources from Hayk, visit: www.haykt. org/mindset-resources

CHAPTER NINE
UPLIFT YOURSELF, UPLIFT EVERYONE AROUND YOU

Goals of This Chapter:

- Learn how to give your best every day
- Discover your daily purpose
- Learn to utilize passion in your day-to-day communication to improve your relationships
- Focus more on your journey and less on the destination
- Understand the Positivity Diet

When you have passion, you have good energy. When you have good energy, you are in a positive state of mind. Even if you're not passionate about what you're doing yet, a positive mindset can jump start you. Passion and energy get other people excited, which in turn adds to your excitement. It's contagious. Passion and purpose can fuel each other. When you care about something, it provides you with a purpose, from that passion, and true happiness can grow.

A lot of happiness can come from the four Fs of your life. We all define the role and importance of each of these in different ways. For example, family can be defined as a group or people you have surrounded yourself with, that you can't live without, something deeper than friendship. They don't necessarily need to be people with whom you share genetics, in fact, they don't necessarily need to be *people* at all. I have seen individuals who have very intimate relationships with their pets. No matter how they fit into your world, all four F's Family, Fitness, Finances, and Friends, have a way of bringing purpose into your life.

I recently watched a YouTube video of a sermon on Discovering your Purpose by John Maxwell[1]. Maxwell is an American author, speaker and a pastor who has written many books focusing primarily on leadership.

When someone asked him, "John, why don't you retire?" His response was, "I have written and sold 25,000,000 books...financially I'm fine to retire, [and] I'm old enough to retire, but why would I? I have passion for what I do, it gives me energy and I have lost myself to my calling. My purpose is bigger than me. I'm having the time of my life when I help others, it's no longer about money, I choose to live till I die, not the other way around".

Having a love for what you do and who you are, is a true key in enjoying the journey in life.

When I say "what you do", I'm not just referring to your career (though that is a big component considering the time spent on it.) I'm also talking about your social circle, your physical wellness, your relationships, your marriage, and your faith. Your daily activities are the foundation of what makes you happy.

The following are some things I worked on myself. I found that with practice, and a mindset shift, I began enjoying pretty much everything I did. This happened naturally, instead of complaining about change, and tasks. While everyone's life always includes a few chores, I no longer do things because I feel I "have" to. I do things because I now "get" to do them. Learning how to look at chores as privileges are a huge part of being in the moment and happy.

When my oldest son David got old enough, I had to change a lot of my morning routine commitments. This meant no more morning cycling, morning runs, and no more writing in the mornings. I was used to getting a lot of my writing done before I got to the office. Since the daycare for David was on the way to my office, it was convenient for me to drop David off at the daycare, then go to the office. Well, between my home and my office there is a freeway called I-405. When I left home at 5AM, I would only spend ten minutes on the freeway, but if I left any later than 6AM I could be stuck in rush hour traffic on the freeway, for an hour. My initial thought of this new "chore" of course was negative. I thought to myself, "I have to now change my morning routine, will have to be stuck in traffic, will have to put up with David screaming in the car, will not be able to listen to podcasts/ audiobooks, etc. There goes my me-time!" The self-complaints were getting out of hand, until I changed my mindset about it, and slowed down, to count my blessings.

At that moment, these were the blessings I focused on. When counting blessings, I also found it useful to think of the opposite scenario:

- I'm blessed to have my wonderful family, I could have been single and lonely.
- I'm blessed to have a business with flexible hours. I could have had a job where my boss would fire me for being late and changing my hours around.
- I'm blessed to be healthy enough to have a consistent exercise routine. There are people who are missing arms and legs or fighting cancer.

- I'm blessed to be motivated enough take on any challenge. Some people struggle just to get out of bed, I jump up when I hear the alarm, eager to take on the day.
- I'm blessed for my son's daycare being so close to my office, it could have been completely out of the way, instead of on the same street in a wonderful city.
- I'm blessed to be in this wonderful country. I could have been back in Armenia struggling to afford electricity.
- I'm blessed that I don't have any major challenges in my life. Plenty of people are fighting battles in their personal and work lives like divorce, harassment, poverty, or illnesses. I don't have anything that keeps me up at night, all my issues are manageable and simple to solve.
- I'm blessed to have healthy children. I know people whose children are sick with leukemia, birth defects, and learning disabilities.

Soon I began to see the problem with my own complaints. I realized that I needed to be more appreciative of my opportunities. I don't *HAVE* to be a good father, I *GET* to be a good father. I don't *HAVE* to be healthy, I *GET* to be healthy. I don't *HAVE* to work hard, I *GET* to work hard. I don't *HAVE* to be stuck in traffic with David, now I *GET* to spend more time with him and teach him how to speak Armenian (and if it's in traffic, so be it!) I really don't *HAVE* to change my morning routine, but now I *GET* to change my morning routine, and take the *opportunity* to be a more supportive husband. Once I turned all of this on its head, I felt great about **getting the privilege** to take my son to daycare, spend some time, laugh and sing with him in the car, and kiss him goodbye before daycare. I was also able to switch my exercise routine and writing times to evenings, and implement office breaks where I would leave from 2-4PM to workout, come back, stay until 5:50 PM, then pick David up at 6PM.

IMPROVING COMMUNICATION TO RAISE THE ENERGY OF YOUR RELATIONSHIPS:

Communication is the process of exchanging information. If information is exchanged properly, then we're all more likely to understand the information being transmitted. Why then do people argue over information? Why is it that we hear answers that can put us on the defensive? Is it because the message was delivered in the wrong way? Was it the tone, or the voice? Or was it because it lacked information?

The answer, is that we are all very emotional and confused beings. We often hear information with the filter we have on at the moment, and that filter depends on the emotion we are experiencing at the time. This is often influenced by the outcome of past experiences. I wasn't the best behaved student in high school, I was better with some teachers than with others. It depended on my synergy with the teacher and their expectations. When I heard my name from a teacher who I knew liked me, I would automatically experience positive emotions, since most times, they would praise me. But when I knew a teacher didn't like me, I automatically felt negative when I heard my name. I felt like hiding, my heart rate would go up, my face would turn red, and I knew I was in trouble. Of course, the teachers that I didn't get along with didn't always call my name for bad reasons, but even if it was a praise, I cringed at the thought of them calling on me at all. I had my mind made up about the scenario before it happened.

The same thing that causes anger in you at one time, may at

another time, create love. The information being communicated may be exactly the same, it might even include the same words, but when delivered in different tones, energy, time of day, mood, and state of mind, it can be perceived completely differently.

I noticed when I improved communication in my personal life, my professional communication improved as well. The two are pretty similar; my business is all about handling questions, objections, discovering prospect needs, servicing clients and communicating with corporate. Being able to have clear conversations, is the bloodline of what we do. I also need to pay close attention to how my *employees* are communicating with clients and I must properly train them to deal with objections. This is what I call the balance of working *in* and working *on* the business. They're different methods but both elements are essentials. Examples of working *in* and working *on* the business are:

- ***In*** business - The owner is either too busy with the business and never takes the time to develop leaders. This limits their ability to grow, or they do the opposite, and start delegating too early and depend on a poorly trained team, leading to failure.
- ***On*** business - The owner leads by example and immediately starts developing leaders based on *who* they are, not what they want. They communicate expectations clearly, and never ask employees to do anything they wouldn't do or haven't done themselves. They spend most of their time communicating leadership, training and developing people, which becomes the bloodline of the business.

My peers and mentors in my business study group, always exchange best practices. One of the main areas of focus we have, as part of *on* the business activities, is actively observing our team.

We assess the combination of, and difference between, quantitative (power conversations, talking fast without paying attention to word count) and qualitative (purposeful conversation - talking slow and less with a lot of attention towards every word and limiting word count) communication. I found one common denominator in disputes or misunderstandings. A *lack of compas! sion* in the delivery tone or approach.

You can have a lack of information that you are attempting to pass on, or you can have too much of it, yet lack quality. The key was the qualitative to quantitative ratio. You may use the best tone, voice and information possible, but deliver it in an off-putting way.

Before I started my business, I cold-called around 29,000 numbers to gather prospects. I didn't have a very thick skin, so this was tough for me at first, but the calls got easier, and I tweaked my communication approach each time. I eventually realized, dialing wasn't the difficult part. The difficult part was recovering from rejections. So, I made rejection the target. I went for ten rejections per day, and began to look forward to the negative calls, as each rejection got me one call closer towards going home. This simple mindset tweak got me to look forward to calling out.

The lesson in dealing with thousands of people that did not want to talk to me was, I learned that the best communication was asking good questions. There are two ways to ask questions, the effective way, and the ineffective way. The problem is when people ask, but don't listen to the answer, because they were too busy talking. The effective way is to ask questions, then listen to, and focus on the reply, versus getting *your* next point across. It can be immensely helpful to use the **WAIT** acronym in communication. You should, ask yourself, "**W**hy **A**m **I** **T**alking?" This is something we could all stand to do more often.

I think I speak for most people when I claim that the phrase, "we need to talk," can strike fear into our hearts. Say this out loud to yourself in an aggressive frustrated tone, as if you're saying this to someone who you're about to start an argument. Now think of someone you want to approach for advice, and say "we need to talk" with a smile on your face. It's the same sentence, of course, but there can be a vast difference in the way people perceive it.

We hear with our emotion. It's often said that human beings are 80% emotional, and 20% logical. Pretty much every self-aware person I shared these percentages with, has admitted that this matches their own experience. No matter how you say things, other people may take offense to them. If they are in a good mood they will hear the good in your message. Since none of us are mind readers, how do we neutralize other people, and deliver information in the way that will be most effective?

As discussed previously, the most important element is to *listen*. If you jump to the answers right away, it can come across as scripted and unnatural. If you permit the other person to speak until they are done, permit them to empty their tank, in other words, then you have an opportunity to deliver your response. Communicate slowly and with the least negative emotion possible. If there is any emotion, it should be a positive one. I used to think that the faster and louder I talked, the more I could say. I thought this would mean that the other person, or people would hear everything. But speed doesn't help to communicate. Rapid loud speaking can actually make you seem *less* competent. I have seen a lot of people power their way through a conversation, without allowing anyone to interrupt, and failing to realize the listening party didn't hear a thing, because he or she was just too busy trying to keep up. Speak in a moderate to low tone so the listener sharpens their ear.

With enough practice, you will become better at reading how people respond to information from you. You will start mimicking them in a way to create the most comfortable situation for them to listen. For instance, you want to match the pace of a slow, collected speaker but still be you. The same goes for encountering a fast-talking powerhouse. With experience, you're better able to read the person across from you, so that difficult conversations become something you look forward to, and you no longer try to avoid them.

COMPLIMENTING HELPS NEUTRALIZE SITUATIONS - THE 4 PARTS TO EFFECTIVE APOLOGY

I have had countless conversations about neutralizing an emotional person. When an angry customer calls, when a frustrated individual confronts you, or when your spouse/partner tells you, "We need to talk," these are all situations that put your guard up immediately. Of course, hearing them out helps dramatically, so does feeling empathy for their anger, but it can also be helpful to find something you like about this person (despite their anger). Focus on complimenting what you like to promote, a positive ego driven conversation. It's much easier to get your point across when you've said something nice instead of speaking into the fire. Most people love being congratulated and recognized. When you recognize and compliment someone, you empower that person to discuss the complaint or problem in a more constructive way. Flattery is very powerful in neutralizing anger. It's hard to be mad at someone who sees the good in you. Of course, you don't want to just throw around meaningless compliments. You really have to read the person and focus on something he or she holds pride in.

I was 18 years old during the summer of 2006, and I took a car salesman job at a local car dealership. It was a very cutthroat sales environment. We were all locked up in a hot office, waiting for people to drive on to the lot so we could jump out, and try to sell them a car. Pretty much the person who yelled out "Up" the fastest when we noticed someone on the lot, would get the turn to go. I got good at keeping a lookout, so I quickly started getting my share of prospects. Within about a month, I started selling a lot of cars, which was good for my paycheck, but bad for the paychecks of the more veteran salesmen.

One time, I yelled, "Up!" a split second before another salesman. Even our manager said I was first, but my coworker did not agree. He came rushing towards me to tell me how much he didn't like me, and accused me of stealing his prospect three days earlier. He claimed that the week before that, I ignored him when he yelled "up" before me. He continued to make accusations that shocked me. I was just the new guy doing what the sales manager taught me. Members of management had been telling me I had a promising career with their lot. But something told me not to fight back with this particular salesman. I asked him to step outside with me, so we could talk in private.

As we were walking, he began rolling up his sleeves, apparently under the impression that I wanted to fight him. As soon as we got away from the office building I looked into his angry eyes and said "Hey man, I apologize. I really didn't mean to upset you. Thank you for bringing this to my attention. I had no idea I was being a little too aggressive with taking prospects, and WOW you have an amazing memory with all these details. I wish you would have told me this sooner. You're a patient guy, and I wish everyone was more like you. What can I do to make things right?"

I meant what I said and right away he became compassionate. He told me it was okay, gave me a pat on my back and said "You took that a lot better than I played in my head. There is nothing you need to do. Go help the customer, and just be less aggressive in taking prospects."

This situation taught me that an *e"ective* apology consists of four parts.

1. Apologize
2. Admit your fault
3. Compliment their strength (This is the tipping point of the apology as it can be the difference of the apology working or not)
4. Ask *what* you can do to make things right

It might take a few compliments to realize which one will work for that specific situation. But once you realize which one is working, you'll notice that the other person will start talking about themselves. This is when you know that you have neutralized the moment. Usually a conflict starts with bad emotions, pointing fingers, and blaming someone other than oneself. When we start enthusiastically agreeing, it's a sign of a good mood or positive emotion.

COMPLIMENTING OUT OF YOUR GENUINE LOVE FOR PEOPLE

Complimenting people and concentrating on their positive qualities will help you develop a genuine love for them. If you need some cheering up or attention, try giving a compliment. It will come back to you compounded. My mentor-friend Ali does this without realizing it. Over time, I discovered that this was the reason I always feel so good around him. He only sees the good in me, and always brings it up in a genuine way. When he knew I was training for my first marathon and wanted to lose weight, he would regularly point out how much better I looked each time he saw me. And while most people just said, "You're losing weight, good job," Ali took that to the next level. He said things like, "Wow! You look great; tell me about your running routine. You're starting to look like a real runner! Keep up the great work." Although I never look for compliments, I never mind encouraging words from people I admire. The people that we're the most comfortable around are the ones that get the best out of us. I can't help but be optimistic when I'm around Ali. Our interactions always result in positive outcomes.

At first, I felt a little odd trying this approach, but after a while it became part of who I am. Now I really enjoy helping promote positive moods in people.

We tend to complicate things by creating mental barriers. Mood is a major component in production figures of pretty much any job, athletics, academics, health, consulting, and sales. Operating in a happy, courageous, and adaptable mood or state of mind, brings good results to pretty much anything you commit to. Think of something you are proud of accomplishing, something associated with hard work, or determination and courageous action. Were you in a negative state of mind when you achieved this? I'm confident you were in positive mindset and a good mood. So, how do you replicate it? If you find it difficult being in a good mood, and maintaining a positive mindset, try teaching it to someone else first. I have found that teaching can really help one master a skill-set. Explaining and breaking things down, requires your understanding first, which will prompt you to do your necessary research on the subject so you are competent when teaching. As you teach, you will also learn things about the subject that you would had never considered learning.

HOW TO CULTIVATE POSITIVITY

Let's use family in this example. Your child gets a written compliment from a teacher. If you provide enough affirmation about what got them the compliment, this will become your child's way of being, and a set a standard for that child to live up to. The reason I say affirmation about "what got them the compliment" and not the "compliment" is because complimenting good results can encourage shortcuts to replicate a result, but endorsing a good process will lead to replicating the good process, omitting shortcuts.

He will remember the positive emotion he felt from receiving the compliment even more than the compliment itself, since emotional memories have the most permanence. Now let's say that your child gets a C grade. You keep reminding him that he needs to improve, and you're speaking repeatedly about that negative result. Although your intentions are good, this will most likely lead to a lower standard, and a negative emotional memory that will permanently mar the moment.

My wife recently started trying new recipes from a website she discovered. I could tell she enjoyed cooking and that it was almost a sort of therapy for her. I also noticed that while trying to spend time in the kitchen, she would stress out over not being able to keep up with the kids and all the other household chores. When I saw that she was getting frustrated, I decided to experiment a bit. Instead of just saying how good the food was, I asked her questions to encourage the "habit". Questions like: How do you find the energy to want to cook after the long day? You really like cooking, don't you? Wow, this tastes good; I bet it's because you cooked with love despite having a crazy day! How do you focus on the task of cooking while having a million other things going on throughout the day? I feel I can't do more than one thing at a time!" As a result, I noticed a dramatic improvement in her attitude towards what she was doing. When we can stay present and not let our mind wander to something else, we are more likely to enjoy the journey. I don't blame my wife for worrying that she doesn't have enough time to get everything done, or ruminating on what she could have done differently. We get tense when we focus intently on accomplishing a task, but if we focus on the enjoyable process, that's where our best, most organized and patient self comes out.

Anything that you do in a present state of mind, leads to a good mood and good results. I shared with my wife what I was doing, and now she does this to me when I'm recovering from a long day. It was no longer about us feeling the need or pressure to take care of each other and our kids, it became more of a positive habit and good experience to look forward to.

THE RITZ CARLTON FRANCHISE 10/5 RULE

I came across this article on a very easy implementation of positive mood technique[2]. The Ritz Carlton is known for their exemplary employee training program. When a staff member is within ten feet of seeing another employee or customer, they make eye contact and smile genuinely. When they're within five feet, they continue smiling and ask how the other person is doing.

When Louisiana's largest nonprofit, academic, multi-specialty healthcare delivery system Ochsner Health Systems adapted this technique, it resulted in a positive 5% increase in patients referring other patients. In addition, doctors who worked for Ochsner were offered better pay positions elsewhere declined offers. When asked why, they responded, "There is something special with the culture of this hospital." This also led to a 40% growth in efficiency in completing projects before deadlines. Employees became more focused, and overall morale and mood positively improved.

If you can follow the Ritz Carlton's lead and use this technique with at least couple of people per day, you will notice more good in people than ever before. There will be more smiles, and more positive interactions, with better conversations and even better relationships. A great deal of good can start with just a smile, even if you have to force it at first. Force it until the habit becomes part of your day. There is one way to know when the habit has been established, it's when it feels awkward to stop. It sounds and can even feel a little cheesy at first, these are the simple changes that can have the most positive impact on what you are looking for from people.

POSITIVE MESSAGES GONE VIRAL

Of course, we're not all positive all the time. We all have our negative moments, sometimes several times throughout the day. When you find yourself feeling, speaking or acting in a pessimistic way, try to stop and figure out what you're thinking about. I bet you will find yourself either reliving something from your past, experiencing a moment of regret, or living in fear about the future. Do the same when you are being genuinely positive. You'll find that this usually happens when you are living in the present. Keep doing this until it becomes second nature to you, and you can do it without having to stop to think. Don't just practice, practice with purpose. As Vince Lombardi once said *"Practice does not make it perfect, practice makes it permanent. Only perfect practice makes it perfect."*

You might assume that negative messages spread more quickly than positive ones, but research proves otherwise. An interesting study conducted at the University of Pennsylvania by Professor Johanna Bergmann involved three months of email data collection. Researchers discovered that e-mails containing positive content had a significantly higher rate of being shared than emails containing negative content.

Bergmann noticed another pattern. Messages that contained positive *and practical* information, got the highest rate of sharing. These results can be extrapolated to include social media posts, blogs, articles, and more. The congratulations, the marriage, the trophy, whatever it is, good news tends to get more likes than complaints and negative posts. Think of someone you've unfollowed or even disconnected yourself from on social media. I bet it was due to negative posts.

I personally post a lot of positive quotes, stories and notes. I encourage you to try the same, and then pay attention to how it positively impacts your attitude, and the attitude of people around you. It took a while, but after several months of doing this, I realized I had developed a silent but powerful group of followers that seemed to demand that positivity. I started getting messages from business managers, heads of organizations, and other leaders. They told me that they appreciated my posts and used them in their team meetings. One gentleman said, "I really appreciate the motivational quotes you post. I run a sales team and during our meetings I reference your quotes quite often. Please keep them coming." He later became a client of mine and referred a ton of his friends and family to me.

I had only been sharing this motivational content because that's who I am. I genuinely feel good spreading it. I was thrilled that it led, albeit unintentionally, to good relationships and a positive impact on my business. It helped me grow a better customer base, and my employees even started developing positive morale. They began working with lower maintenance and easily manageable clients. That is truly, as close to "a perfect client" as you can get. I even noticed that some people were so bothered by my positivity that they *stopped* following me, which was fine by me.

Positivity is like an extremely healthy, difficult to cook, hard to peel, super-vegetable with all the nutrition and vitamins your body needs. You need to spend time learning to cook it properly, and in most cases, you don't look forward to eating it. The amount of effort required to prep and eat this difficult to eat vegetable makes you procrastinate (positivity takes effort). This is why we resort to unhealthy food so much of the time (negativity comes easy). Unhealthy food tastes good, and it's easily accessible, cheap. We lack the discipline to prep our own meals, so we go through a drive through or buy other tasty quick meals, and consume foods our body craves. Positivity requires the extra kind of effort that preparing healthy food does. Our body craves negativity the way we crave junk food. However, just because we crave it does not mean it's good for us. If we can stay positive for a while, it becomes incrementally easier to stay on the positivity diet. Eventually, we see the results kick in, which makes it even easier to stay on the diet. That's the difference between living healthy (positive) or being sick (negative).

You must be kind and generous with your positivity. When you give, you obtain a higher capacity to handle and build more. The more positive you are, the more kindness you can spread to others. With enough kind acts of giving, kindness will become an extremely hard working partner for you. I will expand on this in the next chapter.

To access more tools and resources from Hayk, visit: www.haykt. org/mindset-resources

CHAPTER TEN
YOU ARE A BANK OF KINDNESS

I've found that people who acquire large amounts of success are often unconditional givers. Those are the least selfish, most self-less. Unless you take your eyes off yourself, you will never accomplish anything more than what one person can on their own.

Goals of This Chapter:

- Learn how giving works
- Redefine your purpose
- Accomplish more by doing less
- Learning how you are your best bank, and that self-worth is greater than net worth
- Determining how to "loan" your way out of bad circles
- Make positive change in your life
- Understand how you are your own best credit score

Giving 100% of yourself will help you accomplish quite a bit, but it will never be as powerful as finding a group of like-minded people who will work together and help each other along the way. You can attain *good* results towards your ambitions on your own, unfortunately there aren't that many people that give 100% to themselves. However, *great* results will come when you do a little less for yourself and a little more for others. With the right support group, you can multiply your time, and use that newfound freedom towards what you are lacking the most.

How many of the people that you surround yourself with can you confidently assume are 100% selfish and dedicated towards their success only? These are usually fairly successful individuals that find it difficult to attain fulfillment, as they are lacking the balance in the Four Fs. Then, there are selfish people who save their efforts, maybe for the "perfect time" which may never come. Consistent, focused work requires always being ON and no time to drift off, which is what keeps some people in their comfort zones. It almost becomes an addiction for them to wait for the unknown "right" time in order to give their best. Waiting for all the stars to align to give your 100% effort can over time become an everlasting habit of laziness.

GIVING TO YOURSELF VERSUS GIVING TO OTHERS

A person who only does things for themselves is usually acting out of plain old selfishness. If all you care about is attaining material possessions, it's unlikely that you will be fulfilled or leave behind a legacy and good memories. In my career of being affiliated with a large corporation I have been blessed to be asked to manage other affiliate businesses temporarily until they find and pass the ownership to the next candidate. This process could often take a year. This was always great because I got paid generously for doing only a little more work. One of those offices was owned by my peer Cliff with whom I'd developed a close relationship. Cliff decided to retire on short notice. This merging required me to take over payroll of the existing team, take over the lease, bills, furniture and other basic acquisition items. Naturally when you do a lot of business with someone, you get into deep conversations as you have a lot in common. Cliff is twice my age and has twice as much wisdom as I do, so I loved hearing about his experiences as a business owner.

When I was in his office the last week of his ownership, we were discussing his retirement, and he said to me, "Please don't do what my father and some of my friends did. Please don't focus on selfish thoughts of having more and more money and work yourself to death. Every single one of my friends that did that, accomplished one thing, they all created wealthy, lonely and unfulfilled widows."

You'll have made your way through life without touching others or making a difference. Life's purpose is never about the materials you gain along the way; it's the people's lives you touch along the journey to being your absolute best. It is crucially important to grow relationships that can pick up where your legacy leaves off.

As long as you give unconditionally without any expectation to receive, you will naturally receive from others, often, more than you ever thought you would. People that help others, leaders that create other leaders, people that help develop success, will always have more than they ever gave.

If I spend 100% of my time and effort on myself, I will get exactly what I want out of life. The letter "I" is like the number one, very lonely on its own. But if I give less that means I won't even be a one since it requires 100% to be a one, correct? But that's incorrect. It's a misconception that when you start doing more for others you do less for yourself. It's very important to understand that giving equals receiving with a strong compounded interest. I'm not saying to give and expect back, or give and take. In my experience, it's best to give unconditionally and enjoy giving without any expectations. However, you have to put your efforts in a variety of buckets. When you start focusing on others, obviously you will naturally do a little less for yourself.

WAYS TO GIVE

Let's say that you spend 80% of your time and effort on yourself and spend the remaining 20% on examples I mention below. When you give with a genuine desire to help others, it's only a matter of time before you find yourself surrounded by people who do the same. We all underestimate the power of giving over a decade and overestimate giving for a day. Giving doesn't have to be something you do every day, it can be something you do when the need arises, or when someone asks you for it while being consistent for a long period of time. For example:

- Helping a friend move
- Working out with someone who can use your energy
- Forgiving someone that doesn't deserve it
- Helping more at work and your local church
- When asked a question in any environment, slowing down, educating and teaching versus. giving a short answer just to return to working on what you're working on
- Answering a phone call you don't want to take
- Sending a nice note to a friend you have not seen in a while
- Genuinely smiling when you don't want to smile
- Sending a positive text message
- Replacing a handshake with a hug
- Volunteering at a non-profit
- Breaking to allow cars to get in front of you

- Asking people to count the things they are thankful for
- Telling your parents how much you appreciate them for raising you
- Asking someone what you can do for them to bring value into their day

The examples are endless. If you are looking, you will find the opportunity to give. If you aren't, these openings will simply present themselves as problems and commitments you don't need in your busy life. The Law of Occupancy from Chapter five comes into play here. If the cup is not filled all the way to the top by your will to find a way to give, the empty space will be filled by the opposite, which creates excuses not to. Commitments only work when you can give them your full attention. Kind-of, sort-of commitments usually fall prey to excuses, which are eventually followed by kind of sort of results, and later end up becoming painful regrets.

YOU ARE A BANK OF KINDNESS

When you combine giving and the multiplier of time, you create a network of givers. Most of us are kind-hearted creatures, and none of us like being in debt. If we are, we do what we can to pay it back as soon as possible. Our time and effort work the same way. So, think of yourself as a bank of kindness. Anything you give is never at your loss, it will always be perceived as a loan with interest. When a good person takes your kindness, they will pay you back. Their credibility (like their credit score) is very important to them, so they won't miss a payment or a deadline. After giving several loans of kindness, you will have a large group of people paying you back, both the principle and the interest. Over time, you become a giant financial institution with so much overflow of paid back interest, you start taking that wealth to other places and investing in other products and services and grow your pool of wealth further. A snowball effect, if you will.

People who you give to, will admire your actions, and in most cases, they will do more for you. Now, sometimes it's about finding who *not* to give to. In some cases when you give but get nothing back, the person who you gave, should not have qualified for your kindness loan up front. This means you need to work on your pre-qualification process (that is, you become better at finding who not to give to). Over time, you will attract a lot of good people giving back, often, they've giving even more than you had done for them. As far as the ones that didn't pay back, it's a short-term loss but a long-term gain. Often, the only way to push out the people that you shouldn't have been giving towards is to initially give. Your life's pre-qualification process will get stronger over time, but unless you loan out your time to people, you will not build a list of what to seek and what to avoid.

COMPOUNDING KINDNESS: ACCOMPLISH MORE BY DOING LESS

You might be *so* kind that you give loans to, say, ten people with zero interest. At different points in time, each person received 20% of your effort. After some time passes, you have ten people returning your 20% effort, equaling a 200% effort. This is the compounding feature in action that allows you to accomplish more by doing less.

I really enjoy giving and serving others, it comes almost effort-lessly to me. Though I've been told I let others take advantage of me, I'm ok with that. It's how I filter the "takers" out of my life. I have developed a very good circle of people that are always there for me when I need them. I am usually the first one to help a friend with a move, supporting ideas, encouragement, positive affirmation, supporting a startup, helping friends with fitness goals, volunteering for my community and events, and spreading optimism etc. (although these sound easy it's extremely difficult to do simple easy good things for others *consistently* as anyone can be a one hit wonder).

Therefore, when *I* need help, I feel like I'm overwhelmed with support. When I was moving into another house, my friends got offended when I told them I was hiring a moving company. They insisted upon helping instead. I had a whole crew of friends show up to help me move! When I started a business, most of these friends became clients to support me and even referred new clients. When my wife and I become overwhelmed with the kids, we always have friends volunteering to babysit so we can have date nights. Even in my office, when my team notices I'm behind on something, they do all they can to take stuff off my desk so I can focus on what's important. They even suggest that I leave so I can go to the gym, edit my writing material, or spend time with my family. Going above and beyond has in this way never been in my teams' official "job description," but they do it anyway, because that's how their "boss" is. When other business owners wonder how I find such good employees, my answer is I bring out the good in them through doing good myself *! rst*; not the other way around. Having such supportive people in my life is not a result of luck, it's a result of them knowing I'm always there for them, too. That's how you can accomplish for example 280% (ten people giving back 20% = 200% plus your 80%) worth of work.

That's why I always say "you can't clap with one hand" it's a group effort. I can't say most people, it's all people that are genuinely good people in my life. They're generous, compassionate, and kind. They're the ones I admire and want to be more like, the ones who make a positive difference in other's lives. They're the ones who set an example in the community, they're all natural givers, and giving is second nature to them. Most of them don't even know what they are doing, it's a natural part of who they are.

In Chapter six I talked about Levon, who pours his heart and soul out for others, and takes on the tasks of the community. Levon volunteers at church events, and does what he can for the community for no other reason than to him, there is no other way. It's not one thing a person does that defines them, it's how a person does everything. This is why Levon is not just a successful father, husband, friend, and church member, he is also a very successful leader in his career.

If there were more people like Levon on earth, the world would be a better place. While such individuals are rare, I'm thankful I have a few examples in my life that I can take an example from and aspire to be like.

TO SUM UP IMPORTANT LIFE-CHANGING DECISIONS

You should never wait for certain conditions to be kind, or to be your best. There will never be a "perfect time" for a positive, life-changing step. The conditions never come before the mindset, changing your perception has to come first. We often work hard to attain certain "conditions" -- I'll go for that promotion when I have more time-- that leave us feeling exactly the same as we did before attaining them, because we haven't changed our mindset. A change in conditions can bring temporary satisfaction that expires later, taking you back to feeling as you did before the attainment. So take action now, even a small one, because one completed baby step is a lot better than a million adult steps in contemplation.

To access more tools and resources from Hayk, visit: www.haykt. org/mindset-resources

CHAPTER ELEVEN
SELF-INTENTIONAL PRODUCTIVITY AND RISK-TAKING AT ANY AGE

The difference between being busy and productive is the key in achieving great results.

Goals of This Chapter:

- Realize your true potential
- Develop the habit of being intentional in everything you do
- Make sure you are always doing one more thing
- Learn why you should strive to be courageous and take risks
- Help others without disabling them
- Focus your energy and efforts most effectively

I've stated several times throughout this book that you need to be intentional in what you do. But what exactly does intentional productivity mean? If you had to choose between being busy versus productive, I'd hope you'd choose productive. We can even take it one step further and aim for *self-intentional productivity*.

THE +1 ROUTINE

Let's use daily office-related work as an example. I have admittedly said to myself, "I really want a cup of coffee, but I need to earn this break, so let me make this phone call, I have been putting off. That way I've 'earned' this short time away from my desk." I call this the +1 Routine, because it encourages you to develop the habit of always thinking of one more thing you can do before the next task. Implementing it will help you get more done than anyone you know. Of course, like any routine, you must do it until it becomes second nature, and you don't have to think about doing it anymore.

Let's say I've made the call I was putting off and earned my coffee. I also remembered that I have to talk to my co-worker Diana about something, and since she's on the way to the coffee machine, I'll swing by her office so I don't have to make another trip. I have to send some letters out too, so I'll prep them now so I can put them in the mail outbox on the way to Diana's office. Also, I will send this email out regarding a question I have from a peer, so by the time I get back from my break I might already have an answer in my inbox, as it's a quick question.

The discipline of routine tends to move you towards Self-Intentional Productivity (or SIP) mode. You can also bring this habit to the gym, to your home, and to pretty much any chore or errand. I noticed that my daily routine became more productive, and not just in one area, but pretty much everything I was doing. I prep my gym bag before bed so I don't have to do it in the morning. (It also serves the purpose of keeping my workouts consistent since, if I didn't have time in the mornings to pack my bag, I'd opt to skip the gym). I leave items on the table by the door, so before walking out I don't forget anything that I need to take to the office in the morning, including morning snacks for David before daycare. If there was a package I needed to take to the post office, it was already in my car. I also got very good at setting reminders on my cellphone. This allowed me to get a few extra things done before getting to the office, so I'm not distracted by my errands list, throughout the workday.

These little tweaks allowed me to become much more focused and organized. I even created a weekly workout program for myself. Prior to this, I'd never been a person to train by calendar. I tended to "wing it" when it came to my workouts. I had the habit of purchasing marathon or competition tickets at the last minute for the higher price. This got me to buy ahead, which saved me money and allowed me to turn these into planned family events. I learned that healthy habits have a good way of altering unhealthy belief systems.

One caveat is to avoid practicing SIP during quality time with family and friends, prayer, or rest. No matter how productive and purposeful you become, with everything you say and do, you need to reserve *some* time to not be purposeful and intentional at all. We all need that time to block off all activity, sound, even cut off music and just try to think of nothing. This is equivalent to resting our muscles after a good workout. It also takes self-discipline to rest every day. It can help to set aside an hour per day to do nothing. You might think you don't have time for this, but if you are intentional and it's important to you, you will find time. This period of rest and recharging is what allows you to get all those thousands of other things done. Some of the most accomplished people I know allow themselves some sort of "non-productive" time. This was difficult for me, since I was always somewhat obsessed with productivity. But after a while, I learned that my "non-productive" time is when I'm with family, friends, working out or Sunday church service.

This approach may require change. For instance, when I'm preparing for a marathon, I can spend up to 15 hours per week running and training. It can feel like a part-time job. I set a goal to run three miles in under 20 minutes; but no matter how I ran, how long, how fast, or what strength training I did, I did not get faster. I decided to change my diet. I eliminated as much added sugar as possible and ate only clean, organic food. I also implemented some evening training to sleep in the next morning so that I could get more than few hours of sleep per night (at the time my one and three-year-old boys Arman and David just did not want to fall asleep any earlier than midnight. So waking up at 5AM after a long night of Arman's hourly wake-up cries was not fun). I did that for just two weeks, and finally broke my 20-minute barrier for the three-mile run.

Making a change is not about doing more of what you want to improve. It often requires that you experiment with different approaches to your problem in order to be more efficient. If you can practice the +1 routine, you will develop a method that will eventually produce so much free time to do even more, that people will wonder how you get so much done.

Do you already know someone like this? If so, ask them how they schedule and spend their days. Most people that already do this are doing it unintentionally and many have no idea they're even doing it. These are the people that do in a day what others do in a week. I have my best days when I'm feeling like I'm on a roll with SIP, but I catch myself having a hard time slowing down towards the end of my day. (We all have something to work on.)

There are a few potential downsides to becoming extremely intentional and productive. Sometimes we can become so focused on ourselves that we don't notice how the kind of person we're becoming can adversely impact people closest to us. I noticed three major categories I call Enemies as I observed what I was becoming while utilizing the +1 Routine. I also noticed the same pattern in my peers, that were undergoing the developmental and growth phases of their lives. These are the things to keep an eye on while working on your Self-Intentional Productivity.

#1 ENEMY - THE DANGER OF TOO MUCH WISDOM

The failures and setbacks we experience over the years can tend to make us more cautious about certain decisions. We lose our sense of courage, and our openness when it comes to taking risks. It's fine to be *cautiously* optimistic, but there is a fine line between caution and *fear*. You can still approach problems with great energy and high-level functionality, and find hidden opportunities. But approaching a problem with fear tends to put us on the defense. This fear usually stems from a reminder of past failures. It's crucial *not* to let past failures dictate our future. They can always serve as lessons that help us do things differently this time around, but not serve as an excuse for not doing them at all.

#2 ENEMY - LOSS OF INNOCENT COURAGE

The following is one of my favorite verses from the Bible: "Be strong and courageous. Do not be afraid; do not be discouraged." (Joshua 1:9). When I first read it, it didn't really sink in; I was 18 years old and had no experience with the real world. However, I was very *gutsy* and prone to taking risks. Having courage wasn't a problem for me, but now, after over a decade of mistakes and failures, those same risks seemed crazy and unsafe. We tend to get more *safe and conservative* with time. Whether that's the result of hearing too many cautionary tales, experiencing enough difficulty yourself, or just becoming very analytical, I call that last one the *Professor Approach*.

My business management college professor knew pretty much everything about starting and managing a successful business. He discussed planning, structure, hiring, marketing and countless other specifics. In fact, he knew *so* much about the topic that he would never take the risk of starting a business himself. All the knowledge he had, held him back from acting on the very thing he was teaching others how to do. I believe he would have been very successful, but his knowledge of everything that could go wrong kept him from executing it.

Quite the opposite of this, is the young courageous entrepreneur. Without that "professor's" knowledge he is someone who is not afraid to fail and takes all the risks he can. A few years later, that young individual is hiring people like the professor, to work for him. The entrepreneur had so much courage that he had no capacity for fear so when the opportunity came, he grabbed it. When you are courageous and cautiously optimistic, age doesn't have to be a factor. You can learn to improve the innocent courage, mentality with time. Unfortunately, we often hear that we should play it safe and not break the rules. Some rules are set only by your own limited thinking, which inhibits your potential. This is the kind of perspective that focuses on your weaknesses instead of your assets. How will you know what you're capable of, and how you respond under pressure if you simply remain comfortable with what you are? Discomfort and challenge brings out the best in us.

#3 ENEMY - HELPING VERSUS UNINTENTIONALLY DISABLING OTHERS

When we first moved to the United States, I got a good perspective on how limiting, even the best-intentioned help can be, coming from others. We quickly learned that we couldn't rely on others for too long. I learned that if you want something done, you should do it yourself. People are usually busy fulfilling their own commitments. A lot of good people did help, but everyone has their priorities and their own families to support. I also learned that people have a hard time saying "no" to the needy, but they have a harder time executing promises. We had so many nice people willing to help, especially the families that came to the United States a few years before us and were more established than we were. I could tell the genuine care and attention we were getting especially from a very kind Ukrainian family that would invite us over every Sunday. They would make us breakfast, take us to their church and they would bring us back to their house to eat some more, and I had the opportunity to play with their kids. The father of the family would do what he could to take my father to construction jobs for some income, because we had none. He even donated his very old-jalopy but functional Mazda 323 to us. I remember that car like we owned it yesterday. Later on, I remember being so ashamed when father would take me to school in that car. I didn't want any of the kids to know we were poor, so I would ask my father to park far away. After a while when this family found an opportunity for better work in Minnesota they moved away, and we haven't seen them since. That's when I realized we can't depend on others for long. Everyone has their own schedule and no one wants a burden holding them back. Although people are kind and are willing to help, they have their own agenda and we can't become dependents of others. The best asset in help, is to help yourself and become independent of others aid.

It's tough to say "no" when people are in need, however, it's much easier to say "no" than to commit and later regret making that commitment. For instance, I have a lot of relatives in Armenia that I *want* to help, but want to be careful not to do too much. Sometimes I do a lot less than I can because I don't want to enable additional commitment and dependency. I'm a strong believer in the saying, "Give a man a fish and you feed him for a day, teach a man to fish and you feed him for a lifetime." When my relatives in Armenia ask for money to fix their car so they can commute to work, I send money without hesitation. However, I have one cousin whose husband is an artist that seems to think of himself too good to get a job. His art doesn't make much money; but even when they are broke, he just sits home and works on his art. I find it difficult to help someone who is healthy, smart and can get a stable job but simply chooses not to, because he doesn't want to. Often helping someone who just wants you to "give him the fish," so to speak, and doesn't have the desire to learn to fish will engender dependency and come to expect help from you.

Over the years, I became very good at relying on myself. I learned how to speak English, I learned how to work in sales and marketing and I got very good at coaching and motivating. I ran a very profitable entrepreneurship in construction, and then in the insurance industry in my early twenties. I just could not spend the money fast enough, which I never thought I would have in the first place.

I had more than enough to support myself, my parents, my siblings and help family back home in Armenia. I got very good at helping. In fact, I got *so* good that after seven years of doing every-thing for my father, I had a huge problem when my mother, sister and brother could finally join us in the United States. I tried doing everything for them, too. I got my younger brother a job in my office, bought him a car, paid for his expenses, took care of all the bills to the point where my parents didn't even open mail addressed to their names. I took care of all the paperwork since I spoke better English and did all the talking, instead of letting them learn important things like opening letters, calling on statements, tracking money, and using the internet. I don't think my family even understood what bills were the first several years of us all living together. I thought I was helping them by taking all these important tasks on myself, but I was doing the exact opposite.

After a couple of years of supporting and providing a job for him, my younger brother, Albert , who is much more composed and analytical than me, approached me with a concern, that he had become heavily dependent on my help. He was more comfortable not doing things and letting me take care of him. Instead of enabling him and pushing him to be better, I was taking away his ability to realize his potential. If it was an issue money could solve I made sure to take on that burden which was destroying my family's ability to grow its sense of urgency, risk-taking and other ambitious competencies which were the very things that shaped me into who I was. Because my brother was more self-aware than I was, I was very glad he approached me with this conversation. I would have just continued my ways. He was beginning to feel the toll that my so-called "help" was taking on his ambition and motivation. At the time, Albert was 20 years old and an amateur Mix Martial Artist. He was on his way to becoming a professional fighter, with huge potential as a fighter. He never developed true passion for business while working for me. I blame myself for this, since I never pushed him like I did my other employees, and as a fighter he was always stressing about how one wrong move would end his career. He found himself stuck wondering what kind of a future he wanted for himself, since the fight game was too risky and he didn't have any passion for or felt he was incapable of success in business.

I was getting ready to get married. My wife and I decided to buy a place closer to my office, which meant *away* from my family, who depended on me. I explained to my family that I was moving out. While I would still be helping them financially, I was starting my own family and needed to concentrate on that. I asked my brother to start thinking of a career path, because he would not have a long-term career in my business. He was fully capable, the environment just wasn't bringing out the best in him, and it was very noticeable. I didn't want to force my brother into something that he wasn't passionate about.

At first my family didn't take this well, especially my brother. I could tell they felt that I was being selfish and had betrayed them. It was hard on me seeing my family stress out about the separation, and it was very uncomfortable for all of us. They didn't say much to me, but the look on their faces, and tone in their voices, told me more about their disappointment than someone loudly screaming into my ear. However, it was also one of the best things I've done for my family.

DEVELOPING AMBITION AND A SURVIVAL INSTINCT

About two months after that family meeting, something very special happened. My sister Hripsime got married to my brother in law Edgar. They had moved to Pennsylvania to live with his family, about six years prior. An opportunity arose for Edgar and I to purchase a local franchise retail business chain that I had plans of growing across multiple locations. Hripsime and Edgar moved to Washington, as he had purchased a location close to where I lived at the time. Our families were reunited. It was great having my sister living only 30 minutes from us.

When I was in the negotiation phase with the regional director of the company, Albert approached me and said, "I have given this a lot of thought and I really want to build a better future for myself. What I'm doing now is not what I want to do long-term. What do you think about this, instead of you running another business, what if I give running the franchise a shot?" He went on to show he had truly thought it through. "I have learned a lot about running a business by working here, and I am feeling confident in my ability to run this franchise." By then, Albert had listened to dozens of CDs on business and success, in addition to countless hours listening to me preach about it. He knew what he was getting himself into. Without a question, I gave Albert the number to the Regional Director and asked Albert to call and schedule a meeting.

I was so proud to hear this from him and was surprised that it was exactly what I needed to hear at the time. Once he found out that his "helping hand" (aka *me*) was going away, my brother naturally started to think as a *hunter* no longer as a *dependent*, but as a head of a household. Years later, he now owns multiple paid-off stores, and makes more money than any of the competing franchisees, and he's opening an insurance office five miles from my office, the very thing he didn't have passion for years ago. That's when I realized you can develop passion for the very thing you never thought you would, given the right pressure and circumstances. Additionally, his fighting career has reached an elite professional level. He's currently recognized as the number one fighter in the Northwest, all while maintaining his businesses, being a good husband to his beautiful wife Alla, and father to his adorable daughter Mariam.

The moment that fighting was no longer his *only* way to success, his confidence level skyrocketed and his skills have improved dramatically. Each part of his success complements the other and encourages him to continuously develop his abilities as a businessman, friend, family man and athlete. I'm proud of him beyond words. I understand the desire I had to help him to become someone, after all, no one was there for me when I needed the help, so I didn't want him to endure that same struggle. However, I didn't realize my *not* having help is what made me hard working and ambitious, and allowed me to create my own path. These circumstances permitted me to develop the same ambition and the survivor instinct that my brother eventually did.

Of course, it *is* possible to be over-ambitious and take risks to a dangerous extreme. The ideal path is to find balance between taking risks, and practicing too much caution. Let's take a look at why we're sometimes a bit slow to hit the brakes on risk-taking.

2 TYPES OF PAIN SENSORS -PHYSICAL AND MENTAL

Most people are aware that drinking acid can harm and probably even kill you. You have the option to either pour water or acid in a drinking glass before consuming it. I'm confident you will pick the water over the acid. Now imagine your mind as that glass. You have a choice of what to pour into it. Somehow, we allow acid into it without realizing how it gets there. Why do you think we carelessly fill our *mind glass* with irrelevant, useless, negative information that has the potential to harm us?

We become aware of potential harm to our bodies in two ways. The first way is physical. You drink acid, your pain sensors immediately start sending your brain signals, you stop drinking, and suffer the consequences. Usually this results in a visible scar which serves as a reminder, so you don't do that again.

Your second sensor is your mental sensor. -- This sensor unfortunately is extremely slow to give you signals to stop.

Our busy lifestyles have prompted many of us to become *doers before thinkers*. Society trains us to follow, not to lead. This can prompt us to make decisions, just for sake of checking things off our to-do list, without considering the long-term consequences. I believe this practice plays a huge role in the high divorce rates in the country. Our problem solving skills work on an automatic routine of acting without purpose. It can take a long time for us to get to know ourselves. The mental sensor is almost unnoticeable and is never instantly observable. It doesn't kick in and tell you that what you are doing is the equivalent of drinking acid to your mind. Our minds are more resilient than our bodies in this way, they can take a beating for a very long time before giving you signals. This *strength* allows us to *temporarily* ignore painful warning signs that would ordinarily cause you to stop if you were aware of them.

I noticed that several members of my community went through divorces. The statistics I looked up were confusing, but one thing became clear through my research on divorce rates, they are very high, more than half of married couples end up divorced. This led me to start thinking about the people that I knew who divorced, and I noticed a very significant pattern. The problem didn't seem to occur in the exit of the relationship, but the entrance. People were committing too easily to "fixing a problem" without considering consequences. One situation included an unplanned pregnancy. Another couple I knew had been dating for so long that they figured, "well, we might as well." Another rushed marriage, because they were afraid they were missing something. In another situation, one of the partners essentially threatened the other to commit, or they would leave them. There was peer pressure, cultural pressure and the classic, "I need to get married before I get too old." These people were committing to see *if* they could live with each other versus committing because they could not live without each other.

Rushed commitments are often a sign of a risk-inclined mind. If they weren't entirely sure about the reason and they needed the marriage to fix an issue, it always resulted in a divorce. However, when their reason was "I never see myself without this person", they made it work.

So why is this *mental pain sensor* so slow to give us signs that what we are doing is going to hurt us? Because when we try to fix an issue with a long-term commitment, it backfires. It takes time to get to know someone, even if you've lived with them for a long time. Marriage brings out our truest colors. It's never an instant decision to fix a long-term commitment, it's a slow developing regretful feeling only time can bring forth. So what do you need to keep in mind before making serious commitments? There are two things I will urge you to consider.

This is something I remind myself and talk about in the book often.

- Never make a decision about anything when angry.
- Never commit when happy or when there is an ultimatum.

Go back to chapter eight and re-read the section on the type of positive people in your life. Find the right person and ask for their emotionless advice before making your serious commitments.

THE DANGER OF A TOUGH MIND

It's important to practice caution, we don't want to act, and then think later. Although risk-taking is the first step towards great achievement, planning can help that risk become more positively predictive. For example: What is luck? It's the prepared person being in the right place, at the right time, who utilizes the opportunity and gets what we call *lucky*. In the same vein, *unlucky* is simply the unprepared person being in the right place at the right time, who doesn't utilize the opportunity.

For example: I was helping one of my employees start a business. One of the *homework assignments* I gave him was to call as many business owners that owned a similar company in the area, and pick their brain on their best practices, marketing, market demographics, what-to-do/not-to-do, pre-planning advice, hiring etc. He got back to me with some interesting information. He said he noticed a pattern in the businesses' locations affecting their success. Rural areas had more money in it for the business compared to metropolitan areas. He also noticed the top metropolitan business had very similar processes as the top rural business. But the rural areas' top performers were generating close to *twice* the revenue as the top metropolitan ones (this might be specific to insurance and investment brokerage business.)

We dove deeper into details, hoping to make some conclusions about *positively predictive*, or *lucky results*. We found that if you take a good, hardworking, ethical, positive, driven business owners and put them pretty much anywhere, they will do well. No matter how bad the location, they will make it work. BUT when you put the same person in a good location, that organization will explode with revenue and record-setting production numbers. We didn't just notice this in the insurance and financial planning arena, but also in many other industries that dealt with consulting and relationship building with the general public.

Luck or positively predictive results are a result of risk-taking, along with a well-thought-out plan. It is crucial to make good decisions and execute, but if we don't practice caution, we will always be good. However, great results usually include external information like location. Our work ethic will be good no matter where we go, but other factors can help boost this.

Being intentional does not necessarily require more work when looking at the big picture. It is more effort upfront to weigh the odds, ask for advice, and consider consequences, but you will save an immeasurable amount of effort when you don't have to recover from certain unnecessary failures. It is the habit of slowly developing immunity towards letting things just *happen*; boring jobs, bad relationships, poor health, and being in charge of what happens to you. Your decision making ability can keep you down in a pit, or lead you to the top of the highest mountain peak.

You likely don't remember the first step you took as a young child, but odds are you didn't get up and run. It was a new process, a new feeling, and you probably proceeded with caution. This is the same way to get intentionally purposeful and smarter. Be careful about what information you are reading, listening to, following, practicing, as well as the people you are surrounding yourself with, and what/who you are exposing yourself to. Do they push you to be better, encourage you, smack you when needed, and tell you what you don't want to hear? Remember the law of occupancy. If you don't surround yourself with the right people or information, the space will naturally fill up with the exact opposite.

FOCUS ON YOUR STRENGTHS INSTEAD OF YOUR WEAKNESSES (AKA UNLIMITED POTENTIAL VERSUS LIMITED STRENGTH)

I have a few close friends who don't seem to have realized their full potential. One reason for this seems to be that they spend too much time focused on improving their weaknesses, and never fully open the jar of their strengths. It's common to think that you need to eliminate a weakness before growing something you're good at. But the best way to eliminate a weakness is to hone a strength so much, that you only have the capacity to *barely manage* your weaknesses. Don't avoid or ignore your weaknesses, bring them forward one step at a time. Properly directing and controlling where you spend your energy is the key to achieving satisfying results. This is where *masterminding* a group of people working together towards a common goal, can be helpful. Simply try being more active and spend more time with your mentors. Try to work with someone who has weaknesses where your strengths are, and strengths where your weaknesses are so you can complement each other's abilities.

There is a movie called, "The Pursuit of Happyness," where Will Smith plays the main character. If you have never seen this movie, what I will share next will resonate with you, as the movie storyline is very similar to mine. Regardless of my story I recommend that you watch it. It will give you a strong perspective on mind over matter, which is why I'm sharing my experience below.

My situation wasn't as dire as Smith's character's, but we had some similar struggles. The twelve high-quality interns in my class had been chosen from thousands of applicants. We all were guaranteed the businesses as long as we met all of the deadlines, passed all license tests and did well on the reviews.

My fellow interns and I received a corporate allowance for breakfast and lunch that the others used up right away. I would bring my own food or eat the free snacks in class, so I could save every penny to invest into the business, because I was as broke as one could be during that time. I was assigned an executive who was essentially in charge of hiring or firing me. I think part of why he liked me was my 'whatever it takes' attitude, so he gave me an impossible mission which I worked on daily and almost obtained, until I got sick as a dog, and couldn't get out of bed for two weeks.

The executive Dan, who later became my mentor and a friend, asked me to gather names of 2000 people who would be interested in doing business with me. He told me it would be much easier to walk in with a list of interested prospects, versus just a marketing plan. I needed to finish the list in eight months. I bought into the plan and began cold-calling 150 numbers every day, six days per week. For every 150 calls I would make, I would get 10-12 interested prospects. I knew that since I had 32 weeks to gather 2000 names, the math was simple. This meant 62.5 people per week, which I rounded up to 65. I broke the 65 into six days a week, which came down to 11 per day, and so to get 11 I had to dial 150 numbers.

The list consisted of the entire phone book. Construction contractors from the labor and industries website of Washington state, plus door knocking and a purchased cold calling lists. Sometimes, making those 150 calls took me four hours. I was also studying for an investments license exam, and needed to keep up with all the other homework assignments, so I called at every break, including lunch, and would stay after each day of the internship to finish up. I knew my career depended on it. The group would go to happy hour several times per week, and I would always decline their invitations to call and it helped me avoid letting them know I couldn't afford food at restaurants. While a few of them were offended, some actually joined me, and those are the only ones who completed the internship successfully. The internship was eight months long, and about half were gone by month five, and out of six that opened doors for business, only four of us are still around.

My family's house was undergoing foreclosure. The economy had tanked in 2008. My father's construction business took a dive, and my internship income was barely enough to cover mortgage and utilities. My mother's part-time job as a janitor at a local apartment complex paid for food for all of us. My father got a few construction jobs here and there, but the money was never enough to pay the bills. Both mine and my father's credit cards were maxed out. While my father considered filing for bankruptcy, we didn't even have enough money to consult an attorney, so we let the collectors call until they gave up (which also resulted as a lien against our townhome.) My father does not speak any English, so I also had to deal with the credit companies. Later I somehow managed to apply for a loan modification program, and the bank allowed me to skip a few payments. The loan balance had to stay consistent, so we could apply to the state offered loan modification plans.

Receiving foreclosure notices was the worst feeling. Sometimes I would call the bank on my way to class and leave a message for my case manager concerning the foreclosure letter. Often she would not get back to me until a few days later. The bank helped me apply to dozens of different low income government modification programs. But every time I was declined, due to limited funds and long lines of applicants. I often couldn't sleep until I talked to our case manager the next morning. I kept on thinking she'd tell me it was time to pack up and move out.

The foreclosure notices arrived in FedEx overnight envelopes. My family would wait for me to get home after my evening cold calls for me to open them. They didn't want to call and tell me we got another one, while I was focused on making my calls because they knew how important it was for me to meet my quota.

After almost a year of battling the bank, the modification was finally granted. Our mortgage payments were cut in less than half. The bank forgave the second mortgage, and we managed to get a very affordable payment plan. I finally felt as though I could focus on the business without distractions. I was 22 years old at the time, and while I had dropped out of college right before the internship, I had acquired another kind of education. I learned to manage time, manage my calendar, follow up, negotiate, study for complex financial tests, start a business, hire, train, lead, work under pressure, do payroll, pay taxes, and most importantly, stay focused with a whole lot of adversity in the background.

I had met my mentor Ali during this time, since one assignment in the internship was to work in an existing successful business for two months, and prove that we could produce new business in the real world. On the first day of working in his business, Ali called me into his office to have a conversation about his expectations. It became very clear that he was not going to make it easy on me, and was going to help me determine whether or not this was for me.

I remember the conversation like it was yesterday. Ali called me into his office and said (at least how I remember) "Look Hayk, one of the worst things I can do is make this easy on you. When your doors open you don't want to realize this is not for you. I'd much rather see you quit now, when you don't have employees that depend on you, a lease agreement and other expenses.

So you tell me, what are you going to do in order to produce business? I'm not about to give you any of my customers, and all my new leads go to my existing sales team." I looked at Ali with self-doubt and for a few seconds there, I didn't have an answer. Then an idea came to my mind, so I said, "I have been cold calling for months, and I've gotten very good at it. Why don't you give me a list of all old leads your sales team was not able to get a hold of and I'll start there?" Ali acknowledged that this would be tough, but still said he'd see what he could find for me.

The owners of the agencies my fellow interns were working in let them have access to any file they wanted. They could call existing clients and meet with warm prospects. All of them were given a very solid start, and their numbers were much better than mine, the first few weeks. Ali had given me a cold calling list, and a stack of leads his sales team had burned through years ago. The list had names that no one else had been able to get a hold of. I didn't think it was fair, but I love challenges.

This approach helped me become a new client acquiring machine. By the time I finished my term working at Ali's office, I had out-produced all the other interns, and developed a strong client acquisition process and program. By then, I realized exactly what Ali had been doing. I wasn't handed the easy approach the other interns were, and I can't thank him enough for that. When I officially opened for business in September of 2010, his lessons, along with 2,000 names from the lesson from Dan, served me well. I had set a record not just in my group or the state, but the entire six states of the Pacific Northwest zone. I had signed up more new clients than any other agent my first year. The company even gave me an award on stage at a meeting where I was recognized by the company's executive board. It was the best year of my life.

However, I quickly learned that success is a marathon. It is not about the first mile but how to pace oneself throughout the race. Through Ali's coaching, I slowed down and started managing my weaknesses, which included overworking myself and being a boss like figure. I began utilizing my strengths, I learned to work less, with greater results, and became a better leader to my team. I learned that I'm a much better coach than a producer. I developed a great team and spent my efforts on them, instead of spending ten hours per day on the phone. Discovering what my strengths and weaknesses were became essential for my long-term success.

To access more tools and resources from Hayk, visit: www.haykt. org/mindset-resources

CHAPTER TWELVE
SELF-CONTROL OF YOUR "INNER BEAST"

Goals of This Chapter:

- Learn to control and tame your inner beast
- Learn how to use your inner flame to your advantage, instead of letting it burn you
- Know when it is appropriate to switch hats, while remaining true to yourself
- Understand why risk is not risky at all
- Learn why deliberate delegation is key in having more time

Often people want to "get rid" of anxiety, anxiousness, or over-excitement. The types of things that can get our hearts racing. Sometimes, though, these sudden bursts of energy get mislabeled, because we do not know how to control them or because they come at the wrong time. They are not always bad. In fact, I believe that we can harness this kind of energy for huge benefits.

I personally struggle with the ability to pay attention and stay focused on one activity at a time. I have extreme difficulty studying for complex tests. Even while writing this book, my mind has wandered off countless times. I have to catch myself from drifting away, and bring myself back to what's in front of me. I'm confident that a doctor would diagnose me with Attention Deficit Hyperactivity Disorder and prescribe medicine to *mask* my condition. Yet over the years, I've learned to make this a strength instead of treating it as weakness. I've noticed it's actually an advantage in my business, as controlled chaos is part of my everyday life. Waking up early and going for a two-hour run, arriving to my office to multiple calls, client appointments and team questions, works in my favor to be able to juggle so many different tasks at once. Because of this, I am able to accomplish more in a day than most people do in a week. I have trouble focusing on one thing at a time and taking on too much. I have learned to empty my tank by the end of the day so I don't have any bursts of energy later.

Many athletes, like runners or fighters can get their heart rate up to their maximum capacity, seconds before the gun goes off at the start line or the referee yells "fight". Imagine you are standing in the ring thinking of your opponent getting ready to attack you. No matter how much training you've had, you will *always* get anxious right before a fight. Your heart rate will rise, more blood will flow through your veins, and more oxygen will be delivered to your brain and organs. This is your body's way of preparing you for a peak physical performance. This natural biological occurrence is called a "fight or flight" response or *hyperarousal*.

Hyperarousal is a psychological reaction that occurs in response to an expected threatening activity. It doesn't have to be intense physical exercise for your heart to beat faster. Sometimes, our minds can get our heart racing faster than any exercise.

The bursts I refer to above are the body's way of saying that you have energy you need to release and use. I call that the *inner beast* wanting to escape. It's a feeling like the one that an alpine skier has, before he jumps down the slope. He's able to control the energy increase and later, harness it to his advantage with proper control.

Some of us who get these bursts of seemingly uncontrollable energy, never learn to master our inner beast. Instead of seeing it as a potential advantage, we see it as a condition we need to treat.

I used to play on a basketball team. I was sixteen years old at the time. I can remember one particular game where I felt anxious and stressed, but also good about myself, as though I was, *taming the inner beast*. I knew it was my day to shine. As soon as the game started, I scored the first basket. I ran down to the other side of the court, stole the ball, ran back and scored the second basket. The game went on this way for most of the first half. By that time, I had personally scored more points than the entire team we played against. No matter how much or how fast I ran back and forth, up and down the court, I never ran out of energy.

Nowadays, I experience this several times during the work week. These are the days I feel like I'm on a roll. My friends tell me I'm crazy, but on these days I can go for three hour runs in the morning, be extremely productive at the office, then come home and play with my kids. Even my wife asks me, how am I still full of energy. But, as soon as my head hits the pillow those nights, I pass out.

When I *don't* find a way to spend the energy, those are the nights I don't sleep. If I don't have some sort of outlet, my high energy levels keep me wide awake. While I'm sure this is something a doctor's prescription could mask, I chose my own prescription of release.

Think of a moment when you did something unexpectedly amazing. Now, think about a professional with consistently amazing results. It's never someone who just started, it's likely someone who has undergone years of consistent training. They control their energy and put it to good use. Amazing athletes learn to depend on this energy. Without it, their performance is just mediocre. Physical activity has become my best friend when it comes to helping me control my *inner beast*.

I recommend the same for others, and there are various ways to do this. According to an article published by the ADAA - Anxiety and Depression Association of America, exercise works as well as some medications for helping with anxiety disorders[1]. I understand that exercise doesn't fix everything, and in many cases, therapy, medication, and other help is needed. Each person is unique. However, physicians have been known to recommend exercise like running, biking, weightlifting, yoga, hiking, or even playing a team sport, due to the positive influence on one's health. No amount of medicine can over-compensate for an unhealthy lifestyle. Living a healthy lifestyle doesn't mean you can abuse your body with excessive stress and overwork.

After a while, I didn't just learn to control my inner beast, I learned the timing and appropriateness of how and when to apply my different energy levels. If you observe high-energy people, you'll notice that many are extremely hyper and probably all over the place. Odds are, they've struggled with the same ability to learn and control their inner beast. My mentor Ali is a great example of someone who taught me this lesson. He has an extreme amount of energy, hyper personality and high performance while in chaotic circumstances. Through watching and working with him, I learned how self-control works, and when to wear the different *hats* of my personality.

MANY HATS, SAME HEAD

When I first started getting to know Ali, he reminded me of other people of unparalleled influence and intelligence I'd studied, people like Napoleon Hill, Dale Carnegie, Elon Musk, Anthony

Robbins and Zig Ziglar. Ali is successful, charming, funny, and perhaps his most endearing feature is that he wasn't afraid to display vulnerability. I noticed the same pattern in everyone I looked up to in the past or I admire today. For instance, Ali was the smartest one in the room during group dinners. He was always ahead of the rest of the pack when it came to talking about the stock market, investments, inventions, and ideas.

During one particular event, we were discussing investments. The way Ali knows how money works is unmatched. Then, another friend brought up Real Estate, and Ali said plainly, "I don't know anything about Real Estate." While it seems to be as though he has all the knowledge in the world, he cannot know everything - no one can. He knows what he knows and he knows what he doesn't. He never pretends to have answers that he doesn't. I noticed Ali wasn't afraid to laugh or to make mistakes. He never held back from letting others take the limelight. Although he had the accomplishments to carry himself as a serious businessman, perhaps even talk down to people, he never did. He knew exactly when to take one hat off and wear another, whether it was being a father one second, to a serious CEO the next. Being an expert, tough negotiator one second, to a modest coach to vent to, the next. With all the different hats he wore, he never forgets who he is, or what he stands for, Ali is an unconditionally good human being, with his values in the right order.

The more I got to know Ali, the more amazing things I learned from him. I always assumed that in order to impress people, I needed to share my success stories and accomplishments. Eventually, I learned that it's a lot more impressive when others find out about you without your help, let people see the good in you – don't show them. And learned that you want to get to know someone as a person first, and hear about their accomplishments later. Ali's track record in industries from science, business, invention, academics, and relationships is amazing, yet he never brags.

He simply shares his passion and accomplishments when appropriate. One time, I saw a magazine in his office titled MENSA, and asked him what it was. He told me that he was a member of this organization, but he didn't tell me anything else. I had to probe to find out what the MENSA organization was. I learned that you can only become a member of Mensa when you are in the top two percentile of the Mensa IQ score, which essentially means, you're a genius. Yet, Ali was so modest when explaining the test and telling me how he only missed one answer, which he could argue was the right answer.

Ali appeared to be extremely serious when I first met him. For a while, I thought this was his only side. When I began shadowing Ali, I observed how well he juggled all the different demands placed on him. Every morning when he walked into the office, he greeted all team members and made time to have small talk with everyone, before getting settled. His wife, Jenifer, was the office manager at the time, and she and Ali made a very impressive and successful team. Many other business owners recommend, not to work with my spouse. But thanks to Ali and Jenifer's example, I also now work with my wife.

One day, Ali arrived in a good mood as usual. He got into his office, shut the door and started making calls that didn't sound friendly. Yet, he never lost his cool. It turned out, he was dealing with an employee issue that required him to talk to the employee's parents, and later had to terminate that employee. He didn't share too much with the rest of us. He just said it was unnecessary drama he wanted to keep away from the other employees, and we trusted his judgment.

This experience taught me an important lesson that I use in my own business today. If there is a problem, solve it first thing in the morning. Additionally, if sharing the problem doesn't benefit the rest of your team in any way, just keep it to yourself and learn how to prevent the situation next time.

I am still learning, that no matter how good of a hiring and management process I have, it will never be perfect. Humans are all emotionally driven and inconsistent beings. Ups and downs will always be a part of working with people. But Ali taught me that in order to be a good leader, you have to keep your cool as much as possible, and remain composed regardless of the circumstances.

I've found that a lot of people I admire, and whose philosophies I use, are similar to each other. When I compare Ali to others, I notice something very interesting. Despite the variation of their accomplishments, in different fields (and even in different centuries), I'm always struck by their ability to assess a situation, and know which *hat* to put on, and when.

Ali knows exactly when to take his business hat off and put his family hat on. He knows when to wear his scientist hat, or negotiator hat, or father hat, or inventor hat, or mentor hat. With each one, he exudes so much confidence and authenticity, that he remains the same person. He is too smart to pretend to be someone else.

When I didn't think it was possible to accomplish more, Ali finds yet another hat. He was always fascinated with patents, so when he was in his late forties, an owner of multiple businesses, and a father of two, Ali managed to find time to go to law school.

You might be wondering how he found the time for law school, with everything else he was doing. I know I did at the time! But Ali is extremely good at delegating and having the right people in the right places. He efficiently delegated his duties to his wife Jenifer and his team to take over his businesses. He was willing to make this sacrifice today to earn huge long- term gains tomorrow. That courageous act towards potential gain or loss, is something Ali understands really well. He has helped me understand the risk involved in not taking any risks at all. Taking a risk doesn't have to be a one and done decision if you are intentional in all you do, and make small sacrifices. Small sacrifices such as waking up earlier, showing up earlier and working harder.

My father and his friends threw around a phrase once in a while that I will never forget. "One who does not take risks does not drink champagne." In other words, you will have nothing to celebrate if you never take risks.

To access more tools and resources from Hayk, visit: www.haykt. org/mindset-resources

CHAPTER THIRTEEN
SELF-RESILIENCE IN THE FACE OF FEAR

"Courage is resistance to fear, mastery of fear, not absence of fear." - Mark Twain.

Goals of This Chapter:

- Learn that your limitations are an illusion
- Understand that excuses are like butts, we all have them, and they all stink
- Learn that you can do anything, but some things might take longer than others
- Understand how your future and past, may be adversely impacting your present
- Learn how to use fear to your advantage
- Understand why the line between strength and weakness is paper thin

NO LIMITS STEVE FERREIRA

I was fortunate to meet a very special person during the time I decided to get back in shape and focus on my fitness. At the time, I followed Jesse Itzler's schedule, from his awesome book, Living with a SEAL. Sleep seven hours, train first thing in the morning for three hours, work seven hours and spend seven hours in the evenings with my family. During my morning workouts, I noticed a young guy in a wheelchair who would consistently show up and work out regardless of all the reasons he had not to.

This young man's name is Steve. Steve has a rare disease called cerebral palsy. He explained that his condition occurred due to a lack of oxygen delivery during his birth, which resulted in mental and physical impairment. He can't walk or stand on his own, has speech impairment and his body is not under his full control and he struggles to speak clearly. I really have to pay attention to what he says as he has a hard time connecting words and pronouncing them.

Yet, Steve has a great perspective on life and doesn't take it for granted. He loves living his life the way the rest of us live, minus a few important physical functionalities. He utilizes his strengths to the max and doesn't complain about his weaknesses. Although I see him struggle getting off and onto his wheelchair, mainly using his arms, he still finds a way to use pretty much every machine at the gym. He's in really good shape. He shared pictures of his progress over the last six months and I was truly impressed because he is very defined and muscular.

Steve makes me think twice about fear and making excuses. Though he was born with great physical challenges, his hard work and determination has allowed him to become more successful than most. He does in a way, make me feel sad about how ungrateful and entitled the rest of us are. We're always complaining about things that really don't matter and blaming others for how miserable we are.

Most of us have no issues speaking, walking, or functioning normally. Yet a lot of us don't utilize what we have as well as someone like Steve, who has more than enough reasons to complain, but chooses instead to be fearless and accepting. Steve has taught me many valuable lessons, one of which is not to ever settle with what I believe to be my reality, but to go for what I want, so I can discover my true potential.

The state of fearlessness is a state of having no needs. When you need nothing, you have everything. Steve doesn't need anything, he's happier with what he has, than most fully functioning people I know. Steve took a huge risk to be happy with the way he is. It was easy and safe for him to be comfortable with what he was given, and be bitter and fearful.

The more I got to know Steve, the more impressed I became of his accomplishments. He's working on a book and has a website. He speaks publicly at local schools which has grown to be a full-time business. Additionally, he's training for the Special Olympics for which he has set records on countless occasions. Seeing what he has accomplished with his limited capabilities, emphasizes the potential the rest of us have, that we often do not realize. Every time I have a difficult task ahead of me, I think of Steve and ask myself, "What's my excuse? I'm sure Steve would have found a way!"

I asked Steve to let me interview him for this book, so I could share his story. His experience speaks to how capable human beings are, and how strong we *can* be, once we eliminate all excuses.

INTERVIEW WITH ONE OF THE MOST POWERFUL PEOPLE IN THE WORLD

Me: It's obvious to me and to others what you stand for. What I'm really curious to find out is, what do *you* think of yourself. Who is Steve?

Steve: I'm a living example of inspiration and overcoming limitations that society sets. I bring a new perspective to living life with, and beyond a disability. My workshops help you gain an understanding of living with a disability or perceived limitation, and rising beyond it. They also address how to overcome bullying mentally, and physically.

I was born in Taipei, Taiwan and was adopted through the Christian Salvation Services. My twin sister was born first and I was born an hour later. I wasn't breathing and had an Apgar score of one and had to be resuscitated. (An Apgar score is measured on a scale of zero-ten, ten means the newborn is in the best shape possible, and zero-three means the newborn is in immediate need of resuscitation.) Then, I was placed in an incubator with an IV connected to my head. When I was three months old, my parents realized I wasn't moving like my sister, so they took me to the doctor. I was diagnosed with Cerebral Palsy.

I'm now a motivational speaker and have spoken at over 30

colleges and high schools across Washington State, at conferences, municipalities and internationally in Taiwan. I'm also an accomplished athlete. I've competed in many sporting events, but I enjoy track and field the most. I began competing in 2007 and broke three records in my first year of nationals. I've been on Team USA three times for juniors and have won two medals while on the team. A bronze medal in 2008 for shot put, and I won a gold medal in discus, in 2010, in the Czech Republic.

Me: I can't begin to explain how proud I am to see someone in your condition to achieve so much. I don't know many fully healthy people that have achieved half of what you have. What are *you* proud of the most?

Steve: I'm most proud of what I'm doing right now. It sometimes feels like a dream. I love speaking about *Living a Disabled Life.* It helps people understand the obstacles that people with disabilities face. But, it also shows that people with disabilities can accomplish their goals, even if it takes them a little longer.

I'm proud of the fact that I established my nonprofit, Beyond Disabilities, and that I'm making a difference in the world.

My new project is a workshop on *Eradicating Bullying*. Bullying is an important topic throughout the world, and it needs to stop.

Me: It is obvious that you don't let failure define you, and that you've turned all of your so-called *weaknesses* into strengths. You seem to have a, *no excuses and no limits* attitude towards life, and have demonstrated how tough you are through your actions and achievements. What's your greatest strength?

. . .

Steve: My outgoing personality and my positive approach to everything. It really fires me up when someone says there is something I can't do. I look at that as a challenge, and I love proving people who doubt me, wrong. I'm not afraid to meet new people. I'm comfortable with who I am, and what I have accomplished so far. I choose to be positive and surround myself with good positive people.

Me: It's impressive how motivated you are, and how positively you see everything. Everyone has a fire in them, something that gets them going, gets them out of bed and gets them to want to be great. What motivates you the most?

Steve: Building on what I just said, it's people who have doubted me and proving them wrong. When I was in high school, one teacher told my mom that she was too optimistic to think that I would be able to go to college. Well, I received my Associates Degree from Bellevue College with a concentration in Communications. It may have taken me a little longer, but I persevered and accomplished it. I'm just like any other person. I can do all the things everyone else can. It just takes me longer.

I'm also motivated to help people with disabilities be accepted as regular people. I want disabled people to be motivated to accomplish *their* goals. I have found joy in helping others. While my own accomplishments motivate me, it brings me joy and gives me strength to help and inspire others as well.

. . .

Me: Regardless of their circumstances, everyone, even the most motivated of us, have fears, weaknesses and things that they need to work on. Although you have overcome pretty much every excuse not to accomplish things, do you feel that anything holds you back? What's your biggest weakness?

Steve: My biggest weakness is my fear of being rejected because I'm "different." Most individuals don't think that disabled people are capable of very much. Some even think they're hopeless. This frustrates me. Sometimes I get frustrated that I'm not accepted, or I'm even seen as someone, that people can bully. I tend to focus on this negative moment and not on all the positive people who are in my corner and accept me. There are more positives than negatives, but sometimes the negatives can be hard to overcome. I chose to surround myself with good people, and it is one of my biggest blessings. We keep each other accountable to stay positive.

Me: You have developed a habit of converting problems into opportunities. You don't see negative in what society defines as failure, what other people use to make excuses. How would you define "excuses"?

Steve: Well, this is a hard word to define. In my life, I just try my hardest. When someone says "can't" to me, I ignore this and try to prove them wrong. If I can go to the gym and work out, so can anyone else. How can you say, "I can't" when you haven't tried or tried only a few times and then give up? Unless you have done something so many times that no matter how you attack it, you fail, then there is no excuse for saying "I can't." If you went to the gym and didn't enjoy it the first time, or didn't get the results you wanted immediately, it's because you didn't work hard enough and didn't do it long enough. Excuses are what keep people from achieving their greatness. I have plenty of reasons to make excuses. I simply chose not to.

Me: You shared that you get joy out of helping others and proving to people you can. Is there anything that you do for *yourself* that brings you joy?

Steve: One of my biggest joys, is my motivational speaking. It gives me confidence to live my life to the fullest. I love to motivate people to try their hardest, to accomplish their goals.

Another joy is sports. I have played baseball, wheelchair basketball, wheelchair rugby, swimming, weightlifting, hand cycling and track and field. I love watching and participating in sports. I am aware that I can't live my life for others all the time. Sometimes I'm selfish. I enjoy time to myself. I'm in my own world when I'm working out. It's almost like meditation, knowing I'm strengthening my body and tracking my results. I'm very competitive so naturally I love to set records. It's very cool to me when recognition and awards are involved.

Me: Where do you see all this going? What does a perfect future look like for you?

Steve: My perfect future would be one where everyone is accepted for who they are, and differences do not matter. My long-term goal is to establish a college scholarship program to help kids with special needs. I want to oversee issuing the scholarship, not necessarily to the ones who needs it the most, but the ones who are trying to do the most with what they have. I truly recognize effort, and want to make sure I promote it as much as I can. My own effort has served me well. Although I have to try harder than most and it takes me longer to do what others do, I never lose my will.

Understanding Steve's view on life has helped shape my perspective on my own capabilities. The more I see and interact with him, the more I realize I have absolutely no control over adversity. It will affect us no matter what, so it's up to us to choose whether it positively or negatively influences who we are, and what we do.

While considering this, I came up with an analogy that really resonated with me.

SLOW DOWN AND CONSIDER

Try to recall some thoughts and fears of "what could happen" that you've had either recently, or throughout your life. If you're like me or countless other people I've asked this question, you'll realize that most of these things *never actually happened*. The things that *did* happen, were the very minor concerns that were easy to manage and even ignore, but you were busy letting the bigger fear occupy your mind!

Try this out if you don't believe me. Write down ten things that stress you out and put you in a negative state of mind. Then wait a few weeks. I bet that most, maybe even nine out of ten of those things did not and will never happen. Even that last one that might have occurred is much less excessive than you initially thought it would be.

So why do we spend so much time worrying about things that will never happen?

It's something to think about. Remember, being strong and courageous takes practice. Imagine what today could look like, when we stop living in the fears of the future and end regretting the past! I urge you to catch yourself the next time you are in an extremely good mood. Chances are you are living in the moment.

HOW TO USE FEAR TO YOUR ADVANTAGE (USING A GAS-FUELED CAR ANALOGY)

There were many times in my life where things didn't go as planned. Very often I let the outcome of things that did not go my way, influence pretty much *every* good thought I had. One of my favorite sayings is, "Let your failures re! ne you, it shouldn't de! ne you"- Max Lucado. You can develop a better way to control what I call, your motivational vehicle.

For the sake of this example, let's use the example of a regular gas-fueled car. On the one hand, you have fear, which will always make you believe in what's bad, lack courage and limits your belief system. Then you have faith, which will *give you* courage, eliminate fear, and make you feel as though there are no limits to what you can do. But, one cannot exist without the other. Just as you cannot have a functioning car with just the engine, or just the transmission. The engine will rev, but without the shifting of gears, the vehicle will remain stationary. Below are a few examples to put things into perspective:

SOME EXAMPLES OF ENGINES (FEARS) / SOME EXAMPLES OF TRANSMISSIONS (FAITH)

- Fear of criticism——Courage to express

- Fear of risk——Courage to act
- Fear of change——Courage to embrace change
- Fear of mistakes——Courage to learn
- Fear of failure——Courage to grow stronger
- Fear to settle——Courage to accept what is
- Fear of losing comfort——Courage of discomfort
- Fear of pride——Courage to compromise
- Fear to love——Courage to give love
- Fear to trust——Courage to give trust
- Fear of being great——Courage to realize your potential
- Fear of acceptance——Courage to stand for what's right
- Fear of rejection——Courage of risk
- Fear of friendship——Courage to give and let them take
- Fear of saying no——Courage to tell the truth
- Fear of being happy for others——Courage not to compete against others
- Fear of status——Courage to put yourself below others
- Fear to follow a lead——Courage to accept mentor-ship

EXPLANATION

Our fear of criticism can kill our ability to express ourselves. Most of us know people that we just can't seem to relate to in any way. Maybe it's someone who operates according to a certain belief system, or has a way of doing things that you completely disagree with. Maybe you want to say something but you don't. You might assume they'll figure it out themselves, but they don't. The idea of you expressing your honest thoughts, is dreadful. You don't want to offend them, and you don't want them to reject you, for sharing what's on your mind.

Now, go back and think of a situation when someone gave *you* critique. Maybe they told you to be humble, slow down, don't be loud, wash your hands, smile, be nice, don't judge, quit complaining, work harder or don't be negative. Chances are, you grew from the critique.

Why would you take that opportunity and ability to grow, away from others? If you get a chance to tell someone they need to quit bragging, be nicer, stop being overly competitive, quit judging others, be happier for others, exercise, eat healthier, then do it. You'll get closer to the people you're already close to. The ones in the middle will usually maintain their distance but develop more respect for you, and those whom you aren't very close to, will slowly disappear without you noticing. Sometimes people may stop talking to you when they start respecting you, but that just gives you more time to be with people that matter to you.

Fear of the unknown can lead us to seek safety, and keep us from looking for and developing new relationships. If you don't have any people in your life that you admire and go to for advice outside of your family, start looking. Every person I look up to possesses a quality or qualities that I do not. They've often accomplished something I want, and there's usually a risk factor that led to the outcome, that I admire.

The people I admire aren't just accomplished, they're also very wise. They've learned that if they don't look forward to risk and failure, then they'll need to settle for indifference. No matter what you risk, you'll enjoy one of two positive outcomes, either achieving what you set out to achieve, or learning and becoming wiser.

Relationship development is an important part of both our personal, and business lives. I learned a valuable lesson working with others. An untrustworthy business partner with all the money in the world is worthless, compared to a financially poor but reliable business partner. I've found that being able to put aside my pride has been hugely helpful in developing relationships. This doesn't mean that you should be a doormat, or you should always take the blame. It just means compromise when appropriate. Of course, the appropriateness is the ambiguous part, and requires a unique, case-by-case approach. I see it in the following way. Imagine a scale, one having the least amount of tension, anger and the most amount of love. Imagine the next scale, having the most amount of tension, anger and the least amount of love.

Now imagine you are in the middle of an argument, with your spouse or business partner. There is a good chance you will say something you don't mean, when emotions run high. People often and unintentionally make permanent decisions, while experiencing temporary feelings. When you're in the heat of the moment like this, do a quick assessment of how you are feeling as far as tension, anger and love.

If you rank yourself anything above a five on that scale, then it's time to compromise, recognize the situation, swallow your pride and apologize.

An *e" ective* apology consists of four parts as I explained in Chapter nine.

1. Apologize
2. Admit your fault
3. Compliment their strength (This is the tipping point of the apology as it can be the difference of the apology working or not)
4. Ask *what* you can do to make things right

Learning to let go of pride to find common ground with others, are all part of developing wisdom, which are skills that take time and practice to develop. Of course, when it comes to relationships, this is one that you can't afford to wait, to "master".

There are people in our lives we don't want to experiment on. So be fast in learning to loan people your trust, love, and compromise. Swallow your pride and get good at maintaining the relationships that matter. For the ones that don't pay back, don't loan to them anymore.

Sometimes, we hold back from standing up for something we believe in, or someone who needs it because - as discussed earlier in the chapter - we fear rejection but it shouldn't define you just like it didn't define Steve. This fear never goes away entirely, but the more we flex this muscle, the easier it is to speak our minds. Your real friends will appreciate you for your honesty, and your not-so-real ones will leave, freeing up your time for people that matter. If you have to defend your religion, belief system or understanding of a concept, you need to grow thicker skin and get it off your chest right away. Like the other kinds of failures we've discussed throughout the book, rejection has an ability to strengthen you and open other doors.

In the same vein, it's not your call to take that opportunity away from others. If someone truly needs to hear something from you that you're worried they'll reject, chances are you are doing them a favor by standing up for yourself.

There is a fine line between HCS (Healthy Competitive Syndrome) and UCS (Unhealthy Competitive Syndrome) as I explained in Chapter seven. Both take up a similar amount of energy and time in your life, but they make you feel completely opposite. I went through a phase when other people's success would make me uncomfortable. It made me feel like I needed to do things differently, and prompted me to question the direction I was headed. This was something I discovered as soon as I began making a good living. The more I made, the higher I'd set my bar.

The more financially successful people I met, the more competitive I became. It got to the point that I did not like myself when I was in the company of people who were financially better off than me. I would start boasting, bragging, while trying to top their stories and successes. Thankfully my wife and friends noticed this behavior, and called me out on it - forcing me to change. I am lucky to have people in my life who have the courage to tell me what I needed to hear, and I've grown from them.

It took a while to realize that other people's success is the outcome of who *they* are. It has nothing to do with my outcomes. It took some time and practice, but I learned how to be genuinely happy for other people. Instead of feeling like I had to compete. I began to compliment them and show a genuine curiosity for their success.

I noticed almost immediately that this served to strengthen my relationships, and now those people became more curious about what *I* was working on. Their encouragement and support helped me improve whatever I was passionate about at the time, whether it was my fitness goals, a business idea, or even writing this book. This allowed me to gain support from the very people that I had compared myself to - and whose results I had admired. The difference was just a mindset switch. Stop competing against others, and start being happy for them.

There is a big difference between asking for advice and accepting mentorship. Most people can ask for advice, but very few have the humility required to admit, they need mentorship. But we all need mentorship, even mentors themselves. People can be ego driven beings, so the thought of admitting that there is someone out there who knows what's best for us better than we do, can be a hard pill to swallow. However, none of us will have the opportunity to make all the mistakes we can, over the course of our lifetimes. Learning from others, allows us to skip years worth of mistakes, adversities, issues and get straight to the answers.

We can become geniuses by accepting the fact that we need mentorship, seek the right advice and have the humility to learn from others. When we're too busy trying to impress people, we worry that asking for advice will make us look stupid. Yet, it's *guar‡ anteed* that we'll look stupid, if we don't seek direction from people who know better. Don't worry how things appear to others, to the right person, it's very admirable and impressive when someone asks them for guidance.

Without fear and courage - your engine and transmission -- working together, a vehicle is worthless. Fear revs us up and needs to consume fuel (energy), but in the absence of faith, fear will consume *us*. Faith puts us into the right gear at different times. It regulates and controls how fear impacts our speed at different times. Faith allows us to stop worrying about things we can't control, and be optimistic, that we'll operate in the gear we need. When we get stuck, our faith will guide us into the right gear - even into reverse or neutral. We can't go through life, solely in drive.

Let's also talk a little about the pedals. The gas pedal is your will and your motivation, the brake pedal is your cautious optimism. Looking over your shoulder for a blind spot is your self-awareness. A race car driver needs to diminish his fear of stepping off the gas pedal too early, and braking too early, while maintaining momentum around the corners for the best track times. The driver's thin margin of error, between safety and danger is akin to the closeness between failure and success. If he drives too slowly and safely he will lose; if he drives too fast and carelessly, he'll crash. A consistently good racer doesn't necessarily get the fastest lap time; but he's the one who shows steadiness in speed and safety, and who learns to turn, that is to make a decision, with optimum speed while in the right gear. They brake at the right time while being careful not to step too hard.

Let's look at the track as our life-path over time. When you recognize the proper gears needed for entering a corner, know when and how much to brake, and you know when to step on the gas. The engine will do exactly what you need it to do. But unlike the racetrack, you aren't racing against others in life, instead, you are competing against yourself. As long as you cross the finish line, which is the reason why I wrote this book, you will have a fulfilled life. You only have to understand how all of the components work together. Fear, risk, adversity, difficulties, and bad luck are all part of the journey. Remember, discomfort is something to embrace. Becoming too comfortable means you're likely on the wrong path.

Although it's hard to have everything under control we do have the ability to influence collaboration. As I was writing this paragraph, I looked over at my watch to see the time. I paused for a second and thought, if I remove one part out of my watch, the entire thing will stop working. All of the components work together towards one common goal, to tell time. In much the same way, all the fears, regrets and adversities we face, are part of our daily lives. We must accept them as such, in order to achieve what we want to achieve. It's all part of our mechanism which is built to work together. Understanding the collaboration of all the moving parts is key to a fulfilled and satisfying life.

To access more tools and resources from Hayk, visit: www.haykt. org/mindset-resources

CHAPTER FOURTEEN
SELF-DISCOVERY OVER TIME AND PRESSURE

Life lessons are a mandatory part of the journey that make you who you are. Unless you face and solve certain reality checks, you will not know who you are and what you are capable of.

Goals of This Chapter:

- Develop a new perspective on adversity that helps you discover your true identity
- Take control of life's to-do's instead of your to-do's controlling you
- Examine your relationships and determine which are the most meaningful

We all experience certain lessons throughout the years of our lives. Unfortunately, we also ignore certain lessons, despite how crucial they are for personal development. A lot of times, these lessons are disguised to blend in with adversity.

When I got a call from my brother telling me that he was going to become a father, I sensed a lot of excitement, and a bit of worry in his voice. I don't know who wouldn't be a little afraid of becoming a parent. It involves a great fear of the unknown. Fear of the unknown is the number one killer of execution and courage. It takes away, in one way or another, the sense of comfort and safety we enjoy. For example, when becoming a parent for the first time, we go from living for ourselves, with lots of freedom and a flexible schedule, to following an infant's schedule. We're forced to sacrifice a lot of sources of comfort we have built over time (the most obvious of these being sleep!). The beginning of parenthood is not even a little bit comfortable. But my conversation with my brother was about the forging process of self-discovery. We didn't focus on potential problems that were likely never going to happen.

I told my brother of my experience when my first son David was born. Despite the expected discomfort, the process made me stronger and more disciplined, and improved all areas of my life in drastic ways. I figured out a way to work out in the morning, which meant training myself to be comfortable with around six hours of sleep per night - at the most (something I never thought I could do). I realized how many hours I was spending at the office, so I cut down my work schedule from 55-65 hours per week to 25-35 hours. Somehow, I was able to accomplish more in that shortened amount of time, likely by being more productive and smarter with the time I did have. I made sure my evenings were for family time, and I enjoyed taking Saturday through Monday off business completely.

I explained it to my brother in the following way: "To be honest, Albert, I never would have made these changes on my own. Fatherhood made me become a more efficient person. Sometimes it's not about doing more to become more efficient and harder working, it's about putting yourself through circumstances where you have no *choice* but to improve."

Albert nodded, "I understand, but I feel I'm already really productive and focused. Maybe it will be different for me?"

"Trust me," I replied, "I thought the same thing to myself. And you *are* a very strong and capable person; but that doesn't mean you don't have room for improvement."

"I really hope so," my brother said. "Regardless, I'm so excited to become a dad. Did you really feel you started understanding life better after you became a father?"

I didn't hesitate. "Yes, absolutely. My strengths became stronger. Whatever you think you are good at, efficient at, whatever gives you more energy, and whatever you feel you have perfected, they will all be amplified. Regardless of how strong and good of a person you are, you will become even better. However uncomfortable you've been and however hard you've pushed yourself to improve, this life-changing event will allow you to realize all of your ambitions, and you will be unstoppable. Parenthood made me into a smarter businessman, a better athlete and a better friend. You should look forward to this experience more than anything."

Albert replies, "Thanks, bro. This *does* make me feel good, and excited about becoming a dad. I can't wait for us to all hang out with the kids together like one big family."

Me: "Me too, dream come true."

I would have never made these changes if I hadn't become a father. In this way, parenthood turned me into a better human being. I believed my brother was already a very strong and capable guy, and I expressed this to him. I also felt that this drastic life change would help him understand even better who he was. I assured him that like me, he'd come out a stronger and better person.

HOW TO CONTROL YOUR LIFE TO-DO'S

I hear this a lot from others, they complain that they have too much on their plate, and truthfully, I feel that way sometimes too. No one is immune to adversity. The only real difference in controlling the "life to-dos" and letting them control us, is our approach and perspective. If you *think* things just happen to you, they will. If, instead, you think of them as necessary lessons that you need to experience in order to become a better version of yourself, that's exactly what will happen. You will become better with handling what you consider challenges, and use your experiences to your advantage. You'll become happier with what *is* on your path of self-discovery, instead of fearing what is coming next. I learned this lesson during the early stages of fatherhood.

Sleep was always an important thing for me. I enjoyed a good hard work day as well as a good workout. I always made sure to be so worn out by end of the day, that as soon as I put my head down on a pillow, I would pass out right away. When David was born all that changed. Although what I was doing sounded really uncomfortable to others, it was my comfort having the discomfort of hard work. David was not a good sleeper, he would wake up every hour. Although my wife did a good job during weekdays of putting him back to sleep, I would still wake up from him crying and have difficulty going back to sleep. I had bloodshot red eyes, I was sleepy, low on energy, and my whole day was different because of how tired I was, getting out of bed. I remember the experience being extremely negative. I was just worrying about what the lack of sleep was doing to me. Every time I would hear David cry in the middle of night it would trigger me into a bad mood. When I would come home tired from work, I would get frustrated knowing I couldn't rest and would have to rock him to sleep, feed him and change him. It almost became a chore, that I did not look forward to. I felt I had no choice, I had to do what I had to do. At least this is how it was the first month or so.

After a few months I started developing a deep relationship with David. He began to have eye contact with me. He smiled back when I smiled, giggled when I made funny faces, and his eyes would follow my head movements. I was beginning to fall deeply in love with my little guy, and I realized then, I *don't have* to be up in the middle of night, I don't have to change his diaper, I don't have to feed him, I don't have to clean his puke, or do calf raises while holding him so he falls asleep. I *get to* be up in the middle of the night, I *get to* change his diaper, I *get to* feed him, I *get to* clean his puke and I *get to* do calf raises until my beautiful man falls asleep. It was all just a change of perspective and acceptance of what is.

Everything became clearer and better for me when this change happened in my life. I learned that I *get to* be in traffic on my way to an important destination, I *get to* have a wife that is tired sometimes from busting her tail off for our family, I *get to* be too busy with business because I'm in demand, I *get to* pay taxes because I earn an honest living, I *get to* be overwhelmed because I have a lot of blessings in my life. Happiness is a perspective of a mindset not a condition. The four pillars, Family, Fitness, Friendship, and Finances are not something we're all *entitled* to, they are a *privi! lege* that we get to experience.

WHO ARE YOUR FRIENDS THROUGH THICK & THIN?

If you go back and think of your best relationships, the people who have gone through the good and the bad with you, they're probably the ones with whom you have built the strongest relationships. Most of us, myself included, can count on one hand the number of deep, meaningful relationships we have. Time and so-called struggle doesn't just bring you closer with your partner or friends, it also filters out the people that should have not been there in the first place.

Relationship building has always been difficult for me since I moved so often growing up. I always observed relationships from a non-traditional angle. Even my relationships with my siblings and parents were odd. As I described at the beginning of the book, my father often traveled to Russia for work, when we lived in Armenia. Then when we moved to the US, I was alone with my father for the first seven years. I didn't speak or understand English when we first moved here, and I had a different walk, look, dress code and manners. My father would move us from city to city and state to state. We somehow ended up in Oregon, where we met another Armenian family, and I met Tigran.

Tigran's family wasn't too much better off than us, they were also in pursuit of the "American Dream." Tigran's parents worked hard labor, 60 hours per week just to afford rent and put food on the table. But they had something I dreamed of, their entire family was together, not scattered around continents like mine. In many ways Tigran's sister, Stella, became like my own sister, and his mother was like a mother to me. I would always go over to their apartment to get what I missed so much, a mother's care and older sister's attention. They would make me food and we'd sit around the living room playing video games and having a blast together. We were aware that neither family had much money, but we'd combine a few dollars here from my dad and a few dollars there from Tigran's parents, just to have enough to rent a movie and purchase a few candies at a dollar store, to have our Sunday movie nights. There's no sales tax in Oregon, so a dollar is *truly* worth a dollar at the dollar store. For three dollars, we would get exactly three snacks, usually a bag of chips, trail mix and something sweet like gummy worms. If we had a good week, we'd have a few extra dollars for things like chips and dip.

I was 15 at the time. It had been two years since we moved to

United States and things were going well for me. I was starting to fit in at school, and now I had a friend. However, the construction company my father worked for was moving to do a project in Washington, so we moved again. But I lucked out this time. My father was able to recruit Tigran's father Ruben to Washington, to be our roommates and work for the same construction company. This was tough on me and Tigran.

Starting in a new school and making new friends again wasn't easy. Tigran was also away from his sister and mother for the first time. They had stayed in Oregon so his mother could keep her job at a local bakery and his sister could continue going to the same high school to maintain good grades and apply for college.

Tigran and I were both momma's boys away from their mothers. It was a struggle that helped us develop a deep and meaningful relationship. This shared hardship allowed us to build a better friendship in a short time, than most do in a lifetime. Additionally, the four of us were also living together in a one-bedroom apartment. I pretty much couldn't imagine my life without Tigran, and I'm sure he felt the same way.

After his mother and sister moved into town, they started a business in a neighboring city, bought a house, and began doing really well for themselves. Tigran and I were into success stories and motivational books, by that time. We had fully bought into the American Dream story. Tigran's family took over a small bakery business and applied a lot of what we were learning from the books to make it very profitable. I had a slowly growing construction business, but I wasn't satisfied having only one business. Soon thereafter was when I started my own insurance agency, which became very successful, very quickly. The day my business opened was a tough one, and none of the prospects that promised to do business with me were responding. So Tigran came in on the first day near closing at nine PM after a fourteen hour day, and became my first customer by switching all his family's insurance policies over to my agency. We were both six figure entrepreneurs in our early twenties. We talked every day, worked out together and both supported and represented each other's businesses like they were our own.

Developing a deep and meaningful relationship with yourself is no different than the kind you have with a friend like Tigran is to me. Adversities will bring forth your strengths and leave no room for weaknesses. Things like starting a business, having children, making a commitment or sacrifice don't just test your will, they test your capacity to learn about yourself. Unless you put yourself through tough lessons, your best will never emerge and you may never find out how great you can be. The more tough times I go through, the more I become my best self. This calls for one of my favorite book titles which is also one of my favorite quotes - *Tough times never last, but tough people do - Robert H Schuller*[1].

This is a great read on mental toughness and turning tough times into growth opportunities. It taught me a lot of valuable lessons, and I would recommend this book to anyone looking to learn more on why it's important to be tough.

When I was going through some difficulty, a good friend shared the following quote with me, "Whether you think you can or cannot, you are probably right" - Henry Ford. He was absolutely right. Your belief system defines who you are and how you perceive reality. Learning how to control your thoughts and displaying discipline in your actions is the key to predicting a positive outcome. To get things going, it is crucial to have the right mindset, and positive influence will follow.

To access more tools and resources from Hayk, visit: www.haykt. org/mindset-resources

CONCLUSION

There is no chronological order to living a fulfilled life. The first step is to reverse any unsatisfied part of our lives. This is a change you must initiate from within, in order to live with fulfillment in all four categories of your life, Family, Fitness, Friendship and Finances. Whatever the challenge you're facing, in whatever area of life, ask yourself, "Am I controlling my mind, or are the circumstances controlling me?"

The last thing I want to leave you with, is a secret I discovered over the three years of writing this book.

I've noticed consistent patterns behind successful people. I hear a lot of noise about what the "secret" is, and it isn't just one thing. The following is what it is to me, broken down into four categories:

1. **MAINTAINING A CURIOUS MINDSET** - No matter how successful you already are, or how old you are, maintain a desire for knowledge, and never stop learning. When the desire for knowledge ends, personal growth ends with it.

2. **TIME YOUR DIFFERENT SIDES APPROPRIATELY** - Know how to quickly and efficiently change "hats," or roles, depending on the situation and your audience. We all wear multiple hats. Getting to know each one as well as timing the appropriateness of when to wear each, will save your head on numerous occasions.

3. **LEARN TO MAKE PEOPLE AROUND YOU FEEL GOOD** - Stay modest, humble and kind. Always remain willing to let others have the spotlight. When you do this, people admire you. Maintain your good relationships, and keep good people close, because if you don't, bad relationships will occupy the empty space left behind.

4. **ALLOCATE YOUR ENERGY CORRECTLY** - Know that you need to control your inner beast. We all have it, but we can all control it. Observe the people you admire with high levels of energy, see how they keep their inner beast properly controlled, and allocated in the right buckets. Find what gives you more energy and do more of what fires you up. If you find that certain things drag you down and suck up your enthusiasm and passion, then abandon those things, and allocate your energy into different buckets.

In summary -- love, give, care, be cautiously optimistic, be productive not busy, and value time. Self-worth is more important than net-worth. Look forward to the lessons of failure, stay curious and thirsty for learning, be modest. Remember it's more impressive when people find out about you without your help. Occupy your mind with so much good that

the bad has no room, and most importantly, be you. Never forget you don't control much in life, you only control how you feel with the uncontrollable, and often, how you feel is what brings forth the positive opportunities. Although control is an illusion, you do control your mindset by controlling how you accept what comes your way. Utilize your opportunities to their fullest. Cheers and Blessings to all!

(F4) Formula: Family, Fitness, Finances, Friendships: This formula represents the balance in success. Some can define success as their family; some say it's their health, or the amount of money they have; some even judge success by the number of friends they have. These all are ways of measuring success; however, none will feel truly successful unless there is a healthy balance between all four. To be 100% successful, each tank needs to be split into 25% of the total. When one goes up, the other goes down. It's crucial to not allow money to consume health, relation-ships to consume career, career to consume family and so on.

Compounding Law of Attraction: As in the Law of Attraction, like attracts like, and dislike attracts dislike. Over time, the attraction becomes so strong it almost becomes impossible to reverse. If you are attracting good people, money, and beneficial habits, it consumes and defines who you ardt's no longer about you having a few good friends or one-time success; you have dozens of good friends, endless financial success and a head full of good thoughts and habits. Of course, the exact opposite can compound over time as well, starting from poor decisions all the way down to believing that you're unlucky and lonely and can't do anything about it.

UPR (Unconditional Positive Result): The state of positive outcome. Regardless of whether the outcome is what we wanted to be, the result is always an opportunity. This is the idea of approaching all issues, problems and outcomes as nothing less than an *opportunity*. It requires teaching yourself not to be ignorant to adversity but to look for the good in all bad.

The Law of Commonality Factor: Starting and sticking to your goals is a huge part of succeeding in commitments, but you must make sure you are headed the right direction. If one follows a certain method or direction, the outcome will be close to the most certain predictive future results. For instance, let's say you like the physical build of wrestlers and want to look like a wrestler one day. You will most likely be able to replicate or come relatively close to what they look like if you start exercising and eating the way wrestlers do enough times. In short, you cannot expect the results you are seeking unless you do the similar required work that generated those results in the first place.

UCS (Unhealthy Competitive Syndrome): The unhealthy part of competitive spirit. Although we should all strive to be the very best at what we do, we should also be careful not to allow it to consume us. Unhealthy competitiveness causes people to see victory as the only way; it leads people cutting corners, losing sleep, wanting to beat others instead of getting better for yourself. It is competitiveness for show versus competitiveness for the greater good.

Law of Occupancy: If you pour water halfway into a cup, the cup is half full of water. The space you leave in the cup is occupied by air. That's the part you are not In control of the part you don't fill. Our mind works the same way, if our thoughtsare not 100% positive the rest will be filled with exact opposite which is negative thought.

2+2=4 Formula: No matter how you add two and two, the answer will always be four. The purpose of this formula is to provide an analogy for an unwavering belief system which has worked for you. No matter what others say, you do not change your already-working formula. If hard work has always driven positive results in anything you have done, you do not change your approach or belief system just because someone else got lucky and did it the easy way. You can always try another person's approach, and if their formula's outcome does not match your results, you should go back to your initial belief system.

Self-Intentional Productivity (S.I.P.): This is the state of taking purposeful action at all times. It requires that you have a well thought-out execution plan and only doing things that have predictable results. It means having thought before the action -- not the other way around. The game of chess is a great example; if you are not thinking at least a few steps ahead, you will lose. Strategy is very powerful but can be a difficult thing to grasp. It requires being intentional in all we do every day, every week, and every year.

+ 1 Routine: The discipline to always do one more thing before the next task. For example: I have to use the bathroom, but before I do I need to earn this break so let me make this phone call I have been procrastinating. This way, it's an "earned" trip not an "entitled" one. I also have to talk to my coworker Jon, and since he's on the way, I'll swing by his office so I don't have to make that route again. Since I'm going in that direction, I'll prep these letters I have to send out so I can put them in the mail outbox.

Innocent courage: the act of being gutsy and taking calculated risks. Over time, courage tends to fade away with failure; however, being innocent in courage is about focusing on *new* risk. Sometimes new risk takers that achieve great results are the ones that never thought about the potential downfall of the risk. Innocence is usually dictated by age; that is, the younger a person is, the more open they are to taking risk; the older we get, the more risk-averse we are. Of course, there are exceptions - and examples of very accomplished and smart individuals out there that do their best to maintain their innocent courage. These individuals don't allow reasoning and logic to dissuade them from doing something slightly risky that might pay off. They recognize that sometimes, too much thinking can cause us to be over-cautious and miss out on opportunities.

Helping versus Disabling: The act of doing too much for those who depend on you. Some self-made successful individuals grew up in poverty or less affluent circumstances, and want to provide to their dependents. This might be their children, siblings, parents or even employees. This individual had always wanted someone to help them when *they* were vulnerable; however, they had to figure things out on their own. They likely endured some difficulty, which led them to working hard and wanting to become successful. Naturally this person thinks they're doing the right thing by giving to their loved ones what they didn't have. But they don't understand that it was the *hardship* that made them into who they are. Taking that completely away from the people surrounding brings a sort of learned dependence on others that makes these people very comfortable and saps their own motivation.

Self-bank of kindness: this is the idea of receiving by giving. Becoming a natural giver allows you to achieve more with others' help than you ever could on your own. This approach allows you to eliminate the people who never give back and maintain relationships that will always give back. Being a giving bank is the start to long-term wealth in personal growth and attracting the right people in your life.

REFERENCES

INTRODUCTION

1. ScientificAmericanpublishedonFebruary7,2008writtenbyRobynneBoyd referencing neurologist Barry Gordon at Johns Hopkins School of Medicine in Baltimore. Argument on why we only use a very small percentage of our mind. https://www.scientificamerican.com/article/do-people-only-use-10-percent-of-their-brains/
2. What the eyes see and the ears hear, the mind believes. Harry Houdini Biography Author Profession: Entertainer Nationality: Hungarian Quotes Born: March 24, 1874 Died: October 31, 1926

MY STORY

1. Michael Levine is a publicist, motivational speaker and author of 19 books who has represented Hollywood's most powerful names including Michael Jackson, Bill Clinton, Nike, and Sean "Diddy" Combs. https://www. psychologytoday.com/blog/the-divided-mind/201207/logic-and-emotion

    It is said that emotions drive 80% of the choices Americans make, while practicality and objectivity only represent about 20% of decision-making. Oh, and forget about making a decision when you are hungry, angry, lonely or tried. The acronym "HALT" is exactly the point here: DON"T DO IT! If you make a decision while feeling Hungry, Angry, Lonely or Tired (or God-forbid some combination of more than one of the above) emotion wins 100% of the time and will likely push you in the wrong direction.
2. Anders Ericsson on 10,000 hour deliberate practice concept. http://www.bbc. com/news/magazine-26384712

GET COMFORTABLE WITH THE UNCOMFORTABLE

1. **The Transtheoretical Model**
    https://www.prochange.com/transtheoretical-model-of-behavior-change
2. Harvard Medical School
    Published in March, 2012 *"Why behavior change is hard - and why you should keep trying"* https://www.health.harvard.edu/mind-and-mood/why-behavior-change- is-hard-and-why-you-should-keep-trying

THE 4 PHASES OF CHANGE

1. *The Mind of a Champion*
   Book Author - Julie Bell, PhD, Certified Performance Intelligence Coach and founder of The Mind of a Champion

IMPROVE YOUR FOCUS IMPROVE YOUR RELATIONSHIPS

1. Your brain on multitasking
   https://edition.cnn.com/2015/04/09/health/your-brain-multitasking/index.html
   By Dr. Sanjay Gupta, Chief Medical Correspondent

HOW TO SET S.M.A.R.T. GOALS TO ACHIEVE YOUR DESIRED RESULTS

1. **4 Principles of Execution**
   https://www.franklincovey.com/Solutions/Execution/4-Principles.html

THE COMPOUNDING LAW OF ATTRACTION

1. Law of Attraction: the idea of Like attracting Like: the process that things of matching vibration are brought together, and is the force through which all things were drawn.
   http://www.law-of-attraction-guide.com/history-of-the-law-of-attraction.html

THE POWER OF YOUR WILL

1. *GRIT*
   Author - Angela Duckworth an American academic, psychologist and popular science author.

SELF-DEFENSE WITH POSITIVE THINKING

1. Subjects that would bite diagonally on a pen were happier than the ones who didn't.
   Study by Strack, Martin & Strepper in 1988. www.psycnet.apa.org/journals/psp/54/5/768/

HOW TO ATTRACT THE RIGHT PEOPLE INTO YOUR LIFE

1. *How to Make Friends and In! uence People* Author - Dale Carnegie
2. *The Five Love Languages* by Gary Chapman
   Author - Dr. Gary Chapman a senior associate pastor at Calvary Baptist Church

9. UPLIFT YOURSELF, UPLIFT EVERYONE AROUND YOU

1. John Maxwell You Tube video - Discovering your Purpose https://www.youtube.com/watch?v=lCWCz2QERQY
2. Research about positive thought and how this researched helped retention of employees and clients in large organizations. Ritz Carlton Franchise 10/5 rule and Ochsner Health systems. http://www.servicespace.org/blog/view.php?id=14628

12. SELF-CONTROL OF YOUR "INNER BEAST"

1. Anxiety and depression association of America article on how exercise works as good as some medication to treat anxiety.
   https://adaa.org/living-with-anxiety/managing-anxiety/exercise-stress-and-anxiety

14. SELF-DISCOVERY OVER TIME AND PRESSURE

1. *Tough Times Never Last, But Tough People Do*
   Author- Robert H Schuller an American Christian televangelist, pastor, motivational speaker and author.

ABOUT THE AUTHOR

HAYK TADEVOSYAN

Pronounced - Hike Ta-de-vos-yan

Hayk Tadevosyan is a proud father, husband, deacon, athlete and entrepreneur passionate about serving his community and inspiring others to reach their goals.

Hayk owns and operates a thriving insurance and construction business that he built from scratch. With the years of coaching and developing his top producing teams, he has developed great joy in coaching and consulting other business owners, professionals, aspirants and team members on replicable sales systems, processes of entrepreneurship and personal development.

Hayk brings a unique approach to the definition of success. His inspirational story of perseverance despite the immense odds, has helped him inspire others to grow and achieve the success they've longed for.

Hayk Tadevosyan immigrated to United States at only 13 years of age with his father, having only a few hundred US dollars in their pockets. Since it was financially impossible to bring the entire family to the United States, his mother, sister and brother had to stay in Armenia, a former Soviet Republic, resulting in a 7 year separation of the family.

While the father and son duo slept on roll up mattresses and couches in rooming houses, they often went hungry with only Hayk's provided school lunch available, to feed them both. Hayk developed an unusual fear of new places from all the relocating they did during his childhood years. Moving from city to city, state to state to find work was unavoidable given the circumstances, as it was not an option to skip sending money to their family in Armenia.

From humble beginnings in Armenia, where he lived without the luxury of running water or electricity, often going hungry, to now a successful businessman – Hayk has been described by many as a modern example of the American dream in action.

His first book, The Power of Mindset follows Hayk Tadevosyan's amazing journey from growing up in a poor country of Armenia, to becoming a shining example of achieving the American dream.

Through his experience, Hayk has learned the true meaning of success and is passionate about sharing those lessons. The Power of Mindset includes valuable insights and resources to take back control of our personal mindsets. The Power of Mindset helps us create a better world for ourselves, our families and communities.

Hayk not only shares 14 principles through entertaining and engaging stories that teach how to be successful with family, fitness, friendship and finances, but also what to avoid that may be holding us back from true success and happiness.

Made in the USA
Thornton, CO
08/08/24 10:52:02

01317233-1814-4635-a21d-15b3aef24e62R01